Smart CHOICE

Smart learning—your way, every day.

STUDENT BOOK

3

KEN WILSON | ALICE SAVAGE

OXFORD
UNIVERSITY PRESS

Great Clarendon Street, Oxford, OX2 6DP, United Kingdom

Oxford University Press is a department of the University of Oxford.
It furthers the University's objective of excellence in research, scholarship,
and education by publishing worldwide. Oxford is a registered trade
mark of Oxford University Press in the UK and in certain other countries

© Oxford University Press 2020

The moral rights of the author have been asserted

First published in 2020

2024

10 9 8 7

No unauthorized photocopying

All rights reserved. No part of this publication may be reproduced, stored
in a retrieval system, or transmitted, in any form or by any means, without
the prior permission in writing of Oxford University Press, or as expressly
permitted by law, by licence or under terms agreed with the appropriate
reprographics rights organization. Enquiries concerning reproduction outside
the scope of the above should be sent to the ELT Rights Department, Oxford
University Press, at the address above

You must not circulate this work in any other form and you must impose
this same condition on any acquirer

Links to third party websites are provided by Oxford in good faith and for
information only. Oxford disclaims any responsibility for the materials
contained in any third party website referenced in this work

ISBN: 978 0 19 406129 2   Student Book with Online Practice Pack
ISBN: 978 0 19 406130 8   Student Book Component
ISBN: 978 0 19 406123 0   Student Online Practice

Printed in Great Britain by Bell and Bain Ltd, Glasgow

This book is printed on paper from certified and well-managed sources

ACKNOWLEDGEMENTS

*The authors and publisher are grateful to those who have given permission to reproduce
the following extracts and adaptations of copyright material:* p.23 Dagger DogVinci
text reproduced by kind permission of Yvonne Dagger, www.dogvinci.org

Illustrations by: 5W Infographics pp.33, 53, 61, 88, 100; Mark Duffin pp.69 (snow
scene), 94; Infomen/Début Art p.9; Zhen Liu/Shannon Associates pp.27; Marc
Monés/António Adrião Artist Representative p.110; Geo Parkin/António Adrião
Artist Representative pp.13, 24, 36, 41, 56, 76; Karen Minot pp.83; Gavin
Reece/New Division pp.44, 47, 67, 81; Joseph Taylor/Mendola Art pp.2, 10, 30,
39, 64; Laszlo Veres/Beehive Illustration pp.70, 90, 102.

*The Publishers would like to thank the following for their kind permission to reproduce
photographs and other copyright material:* 123rf: pp.84 (Mia), (Charles/langstrup),
87 (Jeff/Graham Oliver), (Farouk/HONGQI ZHANG), (Sooyun/Leung Cho Pan),
94 (umbrella/Aleksey Telnov), 96 (Mia), (Charles/langstrup), 99 (Jeff/Graham
Oliver), (Farouk/HONGQI ZHANG), (Sooyun/Leung Cho Pan), 106 (umbrella/
Aleksey Telnov), 109 (woman/Ekachai Wongsakul); Alamy: pp.4 (2/DCPhoto),
(4/Paul Carstairs), (5/Hero Images Inc.), (7/EyeEm), 7 (bicycle tour/Wim
Wiskerke), 8 (tropical beach/Aleksandr Matveev), 15 (Chris Hemsworth/
Geisler-Fotopress GmbH), 16 (2/sanga park), (5/dmac), (6/B Christopher),
(8/Mauro La Rosa), 19 (guitar art installation/Hemis), (dog sculpture/Peter
Horree), 20 (JR/dpa picture alliance), 21 (peacock car/Gabbro), 28 (social
networking/Hero Images Inc.), 48 (married couple/GOODLUZ), 49 (Kurt/
Arthur Bargan), 50 (bicycle sign/Goran Bogicevic), (2/Michael Willis), (4/
AztecBlue), (5/Kevin Foy), 55 (Ryo/Image Source), 63 (NYC Highline/Patrick
Batchelder), (Paris River Seine/Hemis), 69 (bigfoot in forest/Dale O'Dell),
73 (robot/Rtimages), 80 (fire and firefighters/Arisha Singh), 86 (cave painting/
robertharding), (oracle bone/Xinhua), (aboriginal/Travel Pictures), 89 (Wendy/
Meibion), 92 (Ariana/Noriko Cooper), 93 (Yonaguni/Nature Picture Library),
98 (cave painting/robertharding), (oracle bone/Xinhua), (aboriginal/Travel
Pictures), 101 (Wendy/Meibion), 104 (Ariana/Noriko Cooper), 105 (Giant's
Causeway/Jorge Tutor), 108 (woman/Tetra Images), 109 (Chapultepec/National
Geographic Image Collection), 111 (community garden/Kathy deWitt),

112 (light in sky/Steve Shuey), 113 (x-ray hand/Science History Images); Getty
Images: Cover: (men's joggin supplies/Yagi Studio/DigitalVision), (birthday
party/Drazen_/E+), (blue background/mfto), (vibrant abstract/mfto), pp.4 (1/
Gabriella Cristallo/EyeEm), 7 (karate/Bobby Coutu), 14 (Worth It presenters/
Rich Polk/Stringer), 20 (art installation in Favella/VANDERLEI ALMEIDA/
Staff), 21 (elephant painting/Jerry Alexander), (comic book cover/Buyenlarge),
29 (women laughing/CHBD), 35 (food being prepared/yulkapopkova), 40 (Key
Largo property/Jeff Greenberg/Contributor), 49 (Mia/Taxi), 54 (pensioner and
child/BSIP), 55 (Sofia/ferrantraite), 60 (cyclist POV/TommL), 64 (flying saucer/
ktsimage), 69 (ghostly figure/gcoles), (cats eyes/Chad Baker), 74 (scientist in
lab/LightFieldStudios), 89 (Ricky/Brian Bailey), (Sangjun/Tetra Images), 94 (old
television/shaunl), 95 (Dr. Amano/Thomas Barwick), 101 (Ricky/Brian Bailey),
(Sangjun/Tetra Images), 106 (old television/shaunl), 107 (Dr. Amano/Thomas
Barwick), 108 (magician/Artrotozwork), 110 (robot/kool99), 111 (woman/
recep-bg), 112 (woman/Juanmonino), 113 (soccer players/Erik Isakson); Oxford
University Press: pp.50 (1/Shutterstock), (3/Shutterstock), 91 (tropical island/
Shutterstock; Simon Dannhauer), 103 (tropical island/Shutterstock; Simon
Dannhauer); Shutterstock: Cover (young man/F8 studio), pp.4 (fitness watch/
Artsplav), (3/Viatkins), (6/Robert Kneschke), (8/Duncan Andison), 7 (woman
sewing costume/Marjan Apostolovic), 10 (retro television/Koksharov Dmitry),
(static noise/panos3), 15 (Beyoncé/PictureGroup), 16 (paintbrushes/Chamille
White), (1/chrisatpps), (3/Hare Krishna), (4/Everett – Art), (7/Slava Gerj),
19 (head sculpture/gg-foto), 21 (woman in fashionable costume/Dan Rentea),
24 (cellphone/Alexey Boldin), (cellphone message/guteksk7), 28 (DiCaprio and
Winslet/David Fisher), 30 (games controller/Vladimir Sukhachev), 34 (people
on cellphones/Iakov Filimonov), 36 (cactus/marijaf), 43 (tablet/bfk), 44 (plaited
hair/Africa Studio), 50 (6/Gang Liu), 55 (Linda/fizkes), 56 (signpost/prapann),
59 (students talking/Motortion Films), 70 (microscope/Steve Collender),
75 (books and sunglasses/GaroManjikian), 76 (microphone/zieusin), 79 (TV
presenter/Gorodenkoff), 84 (Jen/Nadino), (Minseo/siro46), (Eric/AJR_photo),
(Sam/mentatdgt), 87 (Cora/Monkey Business Images), (Olga/Nadino), 96 (Jen/
Nadino), (Minseo/siro46), (Eric/AJR_photo), (Sam/mentatdgt), 99 (Cora/Monkey
Business Images), (Olga/Nadino).

New for Smart CHOICE

Smart learning—your way, every day.

Welcome to *Smart Choice* Fourth Edition. Here's how you can get more involved in your *Smart Choice* lessons:

▶ PRESS PLAY

Watch and learn with **conversation videos** that bring everyday English into each unit.

Feel confident in your learning and explore topics and ideas from around the world with **documentary videos.**

Download all videos from *Smart Choice* at **smartchoice4e.oxfordonlinepractice.com** for access in class, at home, and on the move. Get started with the access code in the front of your book.

💬 GET SPEAKING

OVER TO YOU ACTIVITIES

Have fun learning with new **Over to You** activities! Use the support on the Conversation and Speaking pages to create your own dialogues in English.

SPEAKING AND SMART TALK

Speaking and **Smart Talk** pages in each unit let you practice what you learn with quizzes, games, and real-life situations.

BONUS UNITS

Practice your speaking skills with activities after each video in the **Bonus Units**.

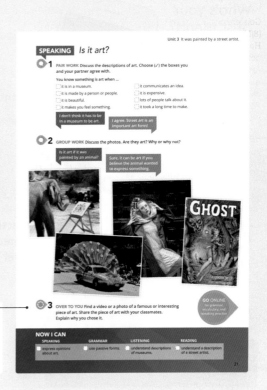

3 OVER TO YOU Find a video or a photo of a famous or interesting piece of art. Share the piece of art with your classmates. Explain why you chose it.

SCOPE AND SEQUENCE

LISTENING	READING & WRITING	SPEAKING	NOW I CAN
People talk about their hobbies	**Reading**: Camera in the Sky **Writing**: An email about your talents (p. 108)	*What have you been doing?* **Smart Talk**: *Personal profiles (p. 84, 96)*	• Talk about free-time activities • Use the present perfect continuous • Understand a podcast about turning a hobby into a career • Understand an interview about aerial photography
Scenes from a show	**Reading**: The Secret to Staying on Top **Writing**: A message about an idea for a project (p. 108)	*The Smart Choice Award* **Smart Talk**: *What do you want to watch? (p. 85, 97)*	• Talk about TV shows and celebrities • Use indirect questions • Understand scenes from a show • Understand how Internet celebrities stay successful
People talk about museums	**Reading**: French Artist Turns Cities into Art Galleries **Writing**: A poster about a public space (p. 109)	*Is it art?* **Smart Talk**: *Art and archeology (p. 86, 98)*	• Express opinions about art • Use passive forms • Understand descriptions of museums • Understand a description of a street artist
People talk about a high school reunion	**Reading**: Friendship in the Modern World **Writing**: A life update for a newsletter (p. 109)	*How did you meet your friend?* **Smart Talk**: *She's the one who ... (p. 87, 99)*	• Describe what people are like • Use relative clauses • Understand conversations about a high school reunion • Understand types of friendships
Reviews of travel apps	**Reading**: Is it Time for a Digital Detox? **Writing**: A product review (p. 110)	*How do you use technology?* **Smart Talk**: *Apps for active people (p. 88, 100)*	• Talk about technology • Use infinitives and gerunds • Understand reviews of travel apps • Understand how a digital detox works
A fictional travel story	**Reading**: Beautiful Beach House **Writing**: The end of a short story (p. 110)	*My travel nightmare* **Smart Talk**: *By the time she was 18, ... (p. 89, 101)*	• Describe events in the past • Use the past perfect • Understand a fictional travel story • Understand an online house rental

SCOPE AND SEQUENCE

UNIT	VOCABULARY	CONVERSATION	LANGUAGE PRACTICE AND PRONUNCIATION
07 Time for a new look! PAGES 44–49	**Physical appearance**	▶ I've had a haircut. **Over to you:** Talk about your appearance.	**Grammar:** *Have / get* something done **Pronunciation:** Reduced vowel /ə/ (schwa)
08 My life would be great! PAGES 50–55	**Features of a neighborhood**	▶ It's a great neighborhood. **Over to you:** Talk about where you live.	**Grammar:** Second conditional **Pronunciation:** Reduction of *would you*
09 What would you have done? PAGES 56–61	**Adjectives to describe feelings and behavior**	▶ He called me Todd! **Over to you:** Talk about an uncomfortable experience.	**Grammar:** *Should have* and *would have* **Pronunciation:** Reduction of *wouldn't have* and *shouldn't have*
BONUS Units 7–9 PAGES 62–63	▶ Growing Cities Talk about the environment and green spaces		
10 Anything's possible. PAGES 64–69	**Mysteries and hoaxes**	▶ It's not real! **Over to you:** Talk about strange photos or videos.	**Grammar:** *May, might, could,* and *must have* **Pronunciation:** Reduction of *have* after modals
11 What would have happened? PAGES 70–75	**Inventions**	▶ It doesn't work! **Over to you:** Talk about a problem with a new device.	**Grammar:** Third conditional **Pronunciation:** Changing syllable stress
12 Did you hear the news? PAGES 76–81	**News**	▶ That's got to be a mistake! **Over to you:** Talk about a news story.	**Grammar:** Reported speech **Pronunciation:** Contrastive stress
BONUS Units 10–12 PAGES 82–83	▶ The Climate Heroes Talk about inventions		

Useful classroom language

1 Listen and repeat.

CONVERSATION

 1 Complete the conversations with the phrases in the box.
Then watch and check your answers.

Can I ask you something?	Do you want to speak for the group?
What does "popular" mean?	How did you answer the first one?
Did you do your homework?	Can you explain it again, please?

1. **A** _Can I ask you something?_

   B Sure.

   A I don't understand this one.

   _____

2. **A** _____

   B For number 1, I wrote "not enough."

   A Really? I wrote "too much"!

3. **A** _____

   B No, but Maria took some notes.

   A OK, I'll ask her.

4. **A** _____

   B Yes, but I didn't do question 5.

   _____

   A It means a lot of people like it.

   B Thanks!

 2 PAIR WORK Practice the conversations with a partner.

01 | I've been running.

SPEAKING
Describing free-time activities
GRAMMAR
Present perfect continuous
LISTENING
A podcast about hobbies
READING
An interview about a hobby

VOCABULARY

WARMUP
What do you enjoy doing in your free time?

🔊 **1** Match the free-time activities with the photos. Write the correct letter. Then listen and check your answers.

a. run marathons	c. make videos	e. ~~draw cartoons~~	g. collect comic books
b. play the violin	d. take selfies	f. do volunteer work	h. go for hikes

 1 *e*

 2 ☐

 3 ☐

 4 ☐

 5 ☐

 6 ☐

 7 ☐

 8 ☐

2 Complete the chart with the words in the box. Then add more words from the pictures.

martial arts   music   yoga   classes   autographs   photos

take ...	do ...	play ...	collect ...
	martial arts		

3 CLASS ACTIVITY Find three classmates who like one of the free-time activities above.

Do you like playing the violin?

Yes, I do. I practice every day.

VOCABULARY TIP

Learn common verb / object pairs.

collect – comic books
     coins
     dolls
do – volunteer work
    martial arts
    sports

CONVERSATION

WHAT HAVE YOU BEEN DOING?

■) 1:32

1 Complete the conversation. Then watch and check your answers. Practice the conversation with a partner.

a. an airline   b. running   c. exciting   d. juice bar

Amy   Ricardo! You look as though you've been **1** _____ !
Ricardo Hey, Amy. It's good to see you! Yes, I'm training for a marathon.
Amy   Good for you! I was wondering where you were. I haven't seen you at the **2** _____ lately.
Ricardo Yeah, I get up pretty early to run before it gets too hot. How are you? What have you been up to?
Amy   I'm good. I have a new job with **3** _____ , so I've been traveling a lot.
Ricardo Cool! Where?
Amy   Oh everywhere, I've been to Japan, Brazil, and Italy this year.
Ricardo How **4** _____ ! You have to take me with you next time.

2 PAIR WORK Practice the conversation again. Use the ideas below. Add your own ideas.

1	2	3	4
working out	coffee shop	an international bank	interesting
exercising	cafe	a tech company	wonderful
_____	_____	_____	_____

3 OVER TO YOU Work in pairs. Make a video of your conversation. Talk about what you've been doing recently.

Student A   Ask your partner what he / she has been doing recently.
Student B   Say what you've been doing and why.

5

LANGUAGE PRACTICE

Present perfect continuous	Grammar Reference page 114
You look as though **you've been running**.	What **have** you **been** up to?
He**'s been running for** almost a year.	**I've been traveling** a lot.
Has she **been working** there long?	**Have** you **been playing** computer games all day?
Not very long. She**'s been managing** their social media **for** only a few months.	No, I haven't. **I've only been playing since** noon.

1 Complete the sentences with *for* or *since*.

1. He's been collecting autographs ___*since*___ he moved to LA.

2. Have you been studying Japanese _____ many years?

3. They've been running _____ hours!

4. Has she been drawing _____ this morning?

5. She's been playing the violin _____ she was young.

6. He's been making videos _____ a very long time.

2 Complete the conversations.

1. A Where _____ you _____ (hide) lately? I haven't seen you around.

   B I _____ (study) Chinese.

   A Oh? Me too! How long _____ you _____ (learn) it?

   B _____ two months. I (travel) _____ there a lot recently, so I need it!

2. A What _____ you _____ (work) on this semester?

   B Actually, I _____ (do) volunteer work.

   A Nice! What kind of volunteer work?

   B I _____ (help) with a community garden.

3 PAIR WORK Give your own responses to the questions in activity 2. Then practice the conversations with a partner.

A Where have you been hiding lately? I haven't seen you around.

B I've been taking art classes!

PRONUNCIATION *Saying statements as questions*

1 Listen to the speaker say the sentences twice. Notice the falling intonation for statements and rising intonation for questions.

1. He's been studying Chinese for a year.

2. She's been sleeping all day.

3. They've been cooking since noon.

4. The kids have been playing all morning.

2 Listen again and repeat. Try to use rising and falling intonation correctly.

LISTENING

1 BEFORE YOU LISTEN Match the photos to the descriptions.

a. He does martial arts.   b. She makes costumes.   c. He plans bicycle tours.

 1

 2

 3

2 Listen to people talking about hobbies. Choose the correct answer.

1. Paco lives in **a city** / **the mountains**.

2. Paco's customers are **tourists** / **artists**.

3. Paco teaches them **photography skills** / **history and culture**.

4. Kristin makes **cosplay** / **historical** costumes.

5. Kristin's customers like to dress up as **superheroes** / **movie stars**.

6. Kristin sells her work **online** / **at conventions**.

3 Listen again. Answer the questions.

1. What was Paco doing when he got the idea for his business?

2. How long has he been doing it?

3. Who does he work with?

4. Where was Kristin when she discovered her hobby?

5. How did the Internet help her with her hobby?

6. How did she get her first customers?

4 LISTENING PLUS Listen to the rest of the show.
Choose (✓) *True* or *False*.

	True	False
1. Kenji got the idea for his business on a high school trip to Japan.	☐	☐
2. Kenji likes karate because it is very competitive.	☐	☐
3. Kenji hopes to help people learn discipline.	☐	☐

5 GROUP WORK Discuss these questions.

1. Who do you think has the best career-hobby? Why?

2. Which hobby would you make into a career?

> I think Paco has the best career-hobby because he works outside and meets people from different places.

SMART TALK *Personal profiles* Student A: Turn to page 84. Student B: Turn to page 96.

READING

1 **BEFORE YOU READ** Look at the photo in the interview. How do you think it was taken?

CAMERA IN THE SKY

What do birds see? Jia Han knows. The 23-year-old **aerial** photographer specializes in using drones to take pictures of the world below. Jia's photos have gained attention in photography **contests**. Recently *PVQ* magazine caught up with Jia on a shoot in Seoul.

PVQ So Jia, how long have you been doing aerial photography?

JH Well, it started with a motorcycle accident. Not mine, but a friend's. She had to stay in bed for a year, so she rented a special drone camera that she could control from her room. I started playing with it and **eventually** got my own. That was about three years ago. I've been using one ever since.

PVQ So what sorts of **landscapes** attract you?

JH I like hills, the way they change shape, and the desert at sunrise.

PVQ Is a drone difficult to **navigate**? It seems like you'd have to make a lot of choices about where to fly to get a good shot. Is that a key skill for the photographer?

JH Definitely. Aerial photographers have a much bigger **range** than people on the ground. We can go 20 meters up or 50, and that decision is really going to affect the picture.

PVQ I'll bet. So what do you recommend for people who are getting started?

JH The ocean. The beach always looks amazing from above, especially a **tropical** beach with all the different blues and whites. I've also seen some beautiful pictures of forests in winter. But artists have to be patient to find that one perfect shot.

PVQ It must be exciting to be one of the first people doing this sort of work.

JH Absolutely! A plane flies too high and too fast to **capture** the details, so this is the first time photographers have been able to show our planet in this way.

PVQ It sounds like you have a real passion for this art form. Thank you so much for sharing.

JH Thank you.

2 Read the interview. Answer the questions.

1. Who is Jia Han?
2. How did she discover her hobby?
3. What is an important skill for an aerial photographer?
4. What one quality is useful for an aerial photographer to have?

3 Match Jia's ideas to the landscape.

1. _____ Jia's favorite type of landscape.
2. _____ Jia admires this type of photo by others.
3. _____ Jia's suggested location for new photographers.

a. Snow-covered trees in winter
b. A tropical beach
c. The desert in the morning

4 **GROUP WORK** Discuss these questions.

1. Where would you take an aerial photograph or video?
2. What other hobbies can you do outdoors?

> I would take an aerial photo of our town.

WRITING Turn to page 108.

SPEAKING   *What have you been doing?*

1 Look at the chart. Have you been doing these activities recently? Add your own idea. Select (✓) the columns that are true for you.

	a lot	a little	not at all
taking photos / making videos			
doing volunteer work			
going to concerts / playing music			
cooking / trying new food			
playing computer games			
watching / playing sports			
_____			

2 **PAIR WORK** Ask your partner if they have been doing any of the activities in the chart recently. How are your activities similar or different?

A Have you been taking photos recently?

B No, I've making videos of my cat. I've been posting them on my social media page.

A How cute! I've been playing computer games a lot. So we are both online, but we have been doing different activities!

3 **GROUP WORK** Play the board game in groups of three.

Each player flips a coin on a turn. Heads move 1 space. Tails move 2 spaces. Answer the questions in the squares to collect points. The player with the most points wins.

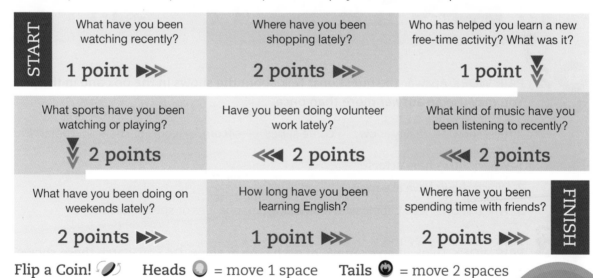

Flip a Coin!   Heads ⚪ = move 1 space   Tails ⚫ = move 2 spaces

4 **OVER TO YOU** Find a photo or video of a free-time activity that requires special skills. Share the information with your class.

GO ONLINE
for grammar, vocabulary, and speaking practice

NOW I CAN

SPEAKING	GRAMMAR	LISTENING	READING
☐ talk about free-time activities.	☐ use the present perfect continuous.	☐ understand a podcast about turning a hobby into a career.	☐ understand an interview about aerial photography.

02 | I wonder what it's about.

SPEAKING
Describing shows and celebrities
GRAMMAR
Indirect questions
LISTENING
Scenes from a show
READING
Staying successful

VOCABULARY

WARMUP
What do you watch on TV or online?

1 Look at the pictures. What kinds of shows are these? Write the correct letter. Then listen and check your answers.

a. cartoon   c. drama   e. game show   g. music video
b. sports program d. news program   f. talk show   h. documentary

2 **PAIR WORK** Answer the questions. Talk about the shows in the box and in the picture. You may use an answer more than once.

| travel show | reality show | crime series | sitcom | cooking show | romantic comedy |

1. Which shows have actors?
2. Which shows have experts?
3. Which shows need people with interesting personalities or special talents?

3 **PAIR WORK** Think of an example of each type of show. Do you watch these shows?

> *Dancing with the Stars* is an example of a reality show. Do you watch it?

> Yes, I do! It's a really fun show.

4 **PAIR WORK** What kind of show would you want to be in? Tell your partner.

> I would like to be a host on a travel show.

10

CONVERSATION

WHAT ARE WE GOING TO WATCH?

▶ 1:32

1 Complete the conversation. Then watch and check your answers. Practice the conversation with a partner.

a. comedy   **b.** try to hide their relationship   **c.** *Mr. Flake*

Maria So, are we going to watch TV tonight?

Amy It depends. I hate trying to decide on a show. There are too many choices!

Maria I know. I've heard this new show is pretty interesting. It's called **1** _____ . Do you know what it's about?

Amy I think it's a **2** _____ .

Maria I wonder if it's any good.

Amy It says it's about two people who **3** _____ .

Maria I'd rather watch that show about the woman who organizes people's houses.

Amy Are you serious?

Maria Why not? It might inspire us to organize this apartment.

Amy If you say so. I'd rather watch someone else clean than do it myself.

2 **PAIR WORK** Practice the conversation again. Use the ideas below. Add your own ideas.

1	2	3
Sunrise Farm	documentary	grow all their own food
Beck & Bosworth	crime series	solve mysteries
_____	_____	_____

3 **OVER TO YOU** Work in pairs. Make a video of your conversation. Talk about what you are going to watch on TV.

Student A Suggest a couple of shows.

Student B Say which show you are interested in and why.

CONVERSATION TIP

MAKING SUGGESTIONS

When you want to make a suggestion, use a rising intonation.

I've heard this new show is pretty interesting.

11

LANGUAGE PRACTICE

Indirect questions	Grammar Reference page 115
Direct	**Indirect**
What's it about?	**Do you know** what it's about?
Why is this show popular?	**Can you explain** why this show is popular?
Who was he?	**Can you tell me** who he was?
What do you want to watch?	**Do you know** what you want to watch?
Is there a game on tonight?	**Do you know** if there's a game on tonight?
What should we watch?	**I wonder** what we should watch.

1 Rewrite the direct questions as indirect questions.

1. What does he like to watch on TV? Do you know ___*what he likes to watch on TV*___ ?

2. Where is that actor from? I wonder _____ .

3. How many channels are there? Can you tell me _____ ?

4. Where is the remote control? Do you know _____ ?

5. What's this show about? Can you please explain _____ ?

2 Rewrite the conversation. Replace the direct questions with indirect questions.

A Is there anything good on TV tonight? _____ ?

B There's a show called Cake Attack.

A What kind of show is that? _____ ?

B It's a baking competition.

A Can you learn baking skills? _____ ?

B Yes, and the bakers have fun personalities.

3 **PAIR WORK** Give your own responses to the questions in activity 2. Then practice the conversation with a partner.

> Can you tell me if there's anything good on TV tonight?

> I think there's a show called ...

PRONUNCIATION *Reduction of do and can*

1 Listen. Notice the reduced sounds of helping verbs *do* and *can* in questions when followed by *you*.

Unreduced	Reduced
1. Do you know what it's about?	/dəjə/ know what it's about?
2. Can you tell me about it?	/kənjə/ you tell me about it?
3. Do you know who he is?	/dəjə/ know who he is?
4. Can you tell me what's on?	/kənjə/ you tell me what's on?

2 Listen again and repeat. Try to say the reduced sounds.

LISTENING

1 BEFORE YOU LISTEN Match each line from a dialog to the correct picture. What kind of show is it?

a. Stay out of the **investigation**!   b. **Arrest** that man!   c. There's been a **robbery**!

1   2   3

2 Listen to three scenes from a show. Match the people to their descriptions.

___ 1. Kitty Cooper   a. a long-time guest at the hotel

___ 2. David Truelock   b. a clerk who works at the hotel

___ 3. Mrs. Vandervault   c. a mysterious figure on the beach

___ 4. Bill Jones   d. a detective on the island investigating a crime

___ 5. A woman with purple hair e. a new guest from New York on vacation

3 Listen again. Complete the sentences with the name of the correct character.

1. _____ has been robbed.

2. _____ tries to calm the victim down.

3. _____ is investigating the situation.

4. _____ hears an argument.

5. _____ finds an important clue.

6. _____ does not want any help.

4 LISTENING PLUS Listen to the ending of the show. Choose (✓) *True* or *False*.

	True	False
1. The inspector has a son and a daughter.	☐	☐
2. Bill Jones is Kitty's son-in-law.	☐	☐
3. The woman's hair provides an important clue.	☐	☐
4. The inspector arrests Mrs. Vandervault.	☐	☐
5. The clerk is the criminal.	☐	☐

5 GROUP WORK Discuss these questions. Then share your opinions with the class.

1. What difficult choice does the inspector have to make?

2. What do you think is the best choice?

SMART TALK *What do you want to watch?* | Student A: Turn to page 85.
Student B: Turn to page 97.

READING

1 BEFORE YOU READ Do you know any Internet celebrities? Who are they?

The Secret to STAYING ON TOP

Steven Lim and Andrew Ilnyckyj

How does an Internet star stay successful? It's hard to compete with newer, younger vloggers, or content producers. However, professional Internet celebrities share certain **characteristics** that have helped them grow and stay popular over time. Here are a few tips that could work for you:

1 Don't be afraid of the camera. Social media stars talk to the audience behind the camera. The British fashion vlogger, writer and entrepreneur, Zoe Sugg, started with a video in which she introduced objects in her bedroom. Her romantic partner, Alfie Deyes, seemed to gain **followers** for his **vlog** just by having an interesting way of saying hello.

2 Experiment, learn, and repeat. Today's successful Internet stars took advantage of **affordable** equipment and online **platforms** to publish content and learn from audience **responses**. The Asian-American filmmaker Freddie Wong produced *Video Game High School* at a very low cost and long before Internet shows became common. Now he has a show about filmmaking.

3 Find a focus. Internet **influencers** generally have a topic. Two friends, Steven Lim and Andrew Ilnyckyj, have built a popular food show. The two young men visit three restaurants and taste the same type of food at different price points. Along the way, they make jokes, talk to chefs, and describe the meal. At the end, they choose the dish that is the best value for the money.

4 Branch out. Stars stay successful through smart **marketing**. Sugg and Deyes started with advertising products. Then they partnered with companies by adding their personality to the story of a product. If you are wondering how they do this, imagine a person with 12 million followers saying they love a brand of make up or clothing. Now they sell their own **merchandise**.

Not everyone can become an Internet influencer. You need to have a nice smile and an outgoing personality. However, the tools and processes for producing web entertainment have made it a dream within reach.

2 Read the article. Match the people to the description.

____ 1. Lim and Ilnyckyj   a. good at creating new business opportunities in the fashion world.

____ 2. Alfie Deyes   b. successful at making a food show more original.

____ 3. Zoe Sugg   c. willing to take a chance on a new way to produce a show.

____ 4. Freddie Wong   d. able to use his voice to gain followers.

3 Read the article again. Write the number of the tip in the article for each example.

____ a. A popular skateboarder starts a new clothing line.

____ b. Two friends sing silly songs in front of a camera.

____ c. An architect travels the world to find the best vacation homes.

____ d. After three unsuccessful shows, a chef gains a million followers when she starts co-hosting the show with a comedian.

4 GROUP WORK Discuss these questions.

1. What do you think: can anyone become an Internet celebrity? Explain.

2. What Internet stars do you follow? Do any of the tips in the article help them stay successful?

WRITING Turn to page 108.

SPEAKING *The Smart Choice Award*

1 **CLASS ACTIVITY** The Smart Choice award is given to a male and female celebrity every year. As a class, choose two male and two female celebrities. Write their names in the chart.

Celebrity	Personality 1–10	Talent 1–10	Influence 1–10	Total
_____				
_____				
_____				
_____				

2 **PAIR WORK** In groups of three, use the questions below or your own to discuss the celebrities.

1. What do you think makes the person a popular personality?
2. Can you explain what the person's talents are?
3. Do you know who the celebrity influences?

> I think Chris Hemsworth has a great personality. In interviews, he makes everyone laugh.

> How about Beyonce? She's got millions of followers and she's so talented.

3 **GROUP WORK** Discuss the celebrities together and then give each person points for their personality, and how talented and influential they are. (1=least, 10=most)

> Awkwafina is the funniest actor alive right now. She should get 10 points!

> I agree. 10 points!

> But she's not the most talented. She should get 7 points for that.

4 **CLASS ACTIVITY** Share your results. The male and female celebrity with the most votes gets the award.

GO ONLINE
for grammar, vocabulary, and speaking practice

5 **OVER TO YOU** Find a celebrity with a secret talent or hobby. Then share the information with your class.

NOW I CAN

SPEAKING
- [ ] talk about shows and celebrities.

GRAMMAR
- [ ] use indirect questions.

LISTENING
- [ ] understand scenes from a show.

READING
- [ ] understand how Internet celebrities stay successful.

03 | It was painted by a street artist.

SPEAKING
Talking about art
GRAMMAR
Passives
LISTENING
Descriptions of museums
READING
A street artist

VOCABULARY

WARMUP
What public art is near you?

1 Look at the photos. What kind of art do you see? Write the correct letter. Then listen and check your answers.

a. sculpture   c. still life   e. drawing   g. installation
b. portrait   d. landscape   f. abstract painting h. mural

 1 ☐
 2 ☐
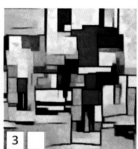 3 ☐
 4 ☐

 5 ☐
 6 ☐
 7 ☐
 8 ☐

2 PAIR WORK Answer the questions. Talk about the words in the box and the words in the photos.

powerful	ancient	graffiti	colorful
photography	realistic	boring	pottery
wild	illustration	statue	traditional

1. Which words are types of art?
2. Which words are used to describe art?
3. Which words can you combine to make new phrases?

VOCABULARY TIP

Learn new words along with specific examples.

sculpture = David by Michelangelo

abstract painting = Bathers by Picasso

3 PAIR WORK What kind of art do you like or not like?

> I like murals because they are often colorful.

> I don't really like landscapes. They are boring!

CONVERSATION

DO YOU KNOW A LOT ABOUT ART?

▶ 1:32

▶1 Complete the conversation. Then watch and check your answers. Practice the conversation with a partner.

a. exhibits   **b.** painting   **c.** colorful

Hannah I like that **1** _____ . What do you think, Diana?
Diana It's a little abstract for my taste. Can you imagine that in your home?
Hannah Yes, it's very **2** _____ .
Diana But look at the price. It's kind of expensive.
Hannah It was painted by Hamish Guthrie. He's becoming quite famous.
Alan Hello, I couldn't help but overhear your conversation. A painting by Hamish Guthrie is definitely a good investment.
Diana Who is Hamish Guthrie? I've never heard of him.
Alan Oh, well, he's a big topic of conversation in the art world these days. He has been called the master of color.
Hannah Interesting. You must go to a lot of art **3** _____ .
Alan I do. Actually, this is my gallery, so it's my job to discover new talent, and Guthrie is one of my greatest finds!

○2 **PAIR WORK** Practice the conversation again. Use the ideas below. Add your own ideas.

1	2	3
landscape	powerful	galleries
portrait	beautiful	shows
_____	_____	_____

↻3 **OVER TO YOU** Work in pairs. Make a video of your conversation. Talk about a piece of art.

Student A Describe a piece of art and how it makes you feel.
Student B Give your opinion.

LANGUAGE PRACTICE

Passives	Grammar Reference page 116
Passive	**Active**
It **was painted** by Hamish Guthrie.	Hamish Guthrie **painted** it.
His paintings **are enjoyed** by millions of people.	Millions of people **enjoy** his paintings.
Was that **done** by a famous artist?	**Did** a famous artist **do** that?
Yes, it was. / No, it wasn't.	Yes, she did. / No, she didn't.
Who **was** that sculpture **made** by?	Who **made** that sculpture?
It **was made** by Michelangelo.	Michelangelo **made** it.

1 Complete the sentences. Use the correct form of the verb in parentheses.

1. The sculptures in *A-Maze-ing Laughter* _____ *were made* _____ (make) by Yue Minjun.

2. Fernando Botero's paintings _____ (sell) for millions of dollars now.

3. Today, most oil paint _____ (produce) in factories.

4. _____ Rodin's *The Thinker* _____ (admire) in France in 1900?

2 Write the words in the correct order to make passive sentences.

1. light / made / installation / was / This / Jung Lee / by

_____ .

2. is / one / the / Picasso / considered to be / of / greatest modern artists

_____ .

3. artists / Japanese / are / by / Many / nature / inspired

_____ .

4. The / every / sculpture / is / by / garden / thousands / of / Brazilians / visited / year

_____ .

3 **PAIR WORK** Rewrite the conversation using passive sentences.
Then practice it with a partner.

A What's your favorite museum?

B The Guggenheim. People visit it from all over. _____

A Did Frank Lloyd Wright design it? _____

PRONUNCIATION *Reduction of* don't *and* did

1 Listen. Notice the reduced sounds of *don't* and *did* when followed by *you*.

Unreduced	Reduced
1. Don't you go there often?	/doʊntʃə/ go there often?
2. Did your father make this?	/dɪdʒə/ father make this?
3. Why did you paint that?	Why /dʒə/ paint that?

2 Listen again and repeat. Try to say the reduced sounds.

LISTENING

1 BEFORE YOU LISTEN Look at the photos. Write the correct letter.

a. an anthropology exhibit   b. a sculpture park   c. a pop culture museum

 1 ☐    2 ☐    3 ☐

2 Listen to the guided tours of three museums in different parts of the world. Match each guided tour to the correct photos in activity 1. Write the correct letter.

1. Guided tour 1 ____   2. Guided tour 2 ____   3. Guided tour 3 ____

3 Listen again. Complete the chart.

		Where is it?	What can you see there?	What makes it special?
1.	The Hakone Open Air Museum			The sculptures change with the seasons.
2.	Museum of Pop Cuture			
3.	The National Museum of Anthropology			

4 LISTENING PLUS Listen to a casual conversation about Brazilian art. Choose (✓) True or False.

	True	False
1. James went to Brazil to see art.	☐	☐
2. Lisa is interested in work by Brazilian artists.	☐	☐
3. Lisa was affected by a powerful exhibit.	☐	☐
4. Lisa says Eduardo Kobra is one of a few street artists in Rio.	☐	☐
5. Lisa hopes to put on an exhibit of art in Brazil.	☐	☐

5 GROUP WORK Discuss these questions.

1. Which museum in the listening would you rather visit? Why?

2. What museums are near you? What do they look like?

> I'd rather visit the Museum of Anthropology. It's the oldest, and it has art and history.

SMART TALK *Art and archeology* Student A: Turn to page 86. | Student B: Turn to page 98.

READING

1 **BEFORE YOU READ** What is street art? Is there any where you live?

FRENCH ARTIST TURNS CITIES **INTO ART GALLERIES**

Around the same time that social media started allowing people to post photos on the Internet, a young street artist began using the public spaces in the world's most dangerous cities as art galleries.

JR, as he is his known, is a street artist who got his start doing graffiti in Paris. One day he found a camera and started taking photos of people he met on his graffiti **expeditions**. After the photos were printed, he **pasted** them onto public walls for anyone to see. In order to make them stand out, he painted brightly colored **frames** around them. Sometimes the photos were taken down by authorities, but the frames remained.

This was the beginning of JR's efforts to display art outside of museums. He was drawn to places of **suffering** and a desire to bring art to people who did not have it. For one of his projects, he printed giant close-up photographs of people who did the same jobs but lived in enemy countries. Then he pasted them side by side on public walls. When people asked him about them, he said, "Can you tell who is who?" And often, people couldn't match a person with a country.

JR's next project was called *Women are Heroes*. He took pictures of women who had experienced **violence**, and he asked men to help **paste** their images on walls, stairs, and even the roofs of houses. Some of these prints were more than six meters tall. Others were printed on waterproof material and used as roofs where they protected people from the rain.

JR also **inspires** others to participate in his projects. He has invited people to send him their own photos. The photos are printed and returned in giant sizes so they can be installed in the photographers' communities. In this way, JR is also inspiring a new generation of artists who can tell their own stories.

 2 Read the article. Answer the questions.

1. Who is JR?
2. What does he do with his photographs?
3. What types of places does he bring his art to?
4. What did JR do for his *Women are Heroes* project?
5. What does he do to help a new generation of street artists?

3 Read the article again. Find examples in the article to support these statements.

Street artists...	Example from the article
show work outside of museums.	
do not always have permission.	
make work that is useful.	

4 **GROUP WORK** Discuss these questions.

1. What do you think of JR's photos on public walls?
2. Who would you photograph if you were part of one of JR's projects? Explain why.

> I think JR's photos are inspiring for certain places, but...

WRITING Turn to page 109.

SPEAKING   *Is it art?*

1 **PAIR WORK** Discuss the descriptions of art. Choose (✓) the boxes you and your partner agree with.

You know something is art when ...

☐ it is in a museum.
☐ it is made by a person or people.
☐ it is beautiful.
☐ it makes you feel something.

☐ it communicates an idea.
☐ it is expensive.
☐ lots of people talk about it.
☐ it took a long time to make.

> I don't think it has to be in a museum to be art.

> I agree. Street art is an important art form!

2 **GROUP WORK** Discuss the photos. Are they art? Why or why not?

> Is it art if it was painted by an animal?

> Sure, it can be art if you believe the animal wanted to express something.

3 **OVER TO YOU** Find a video or a photo of a famous or interesting piece of art. Share the piece of art with your classmates. Explain why you chose it.

GO ONLINE
for grammar, vocabulary, and speaking practice

NOW I CAN

SPEAKING	GRAMMAR	LISTENING	READING
☐ express opinions about art.	☐ use passive forms.	☐ understand descriptions of museums.	☐ understand a description of a street artist.

VIDEO

Bristol Dubwize by Stanstylee

1 **PAIR WORK** What kind of artist is Stanstylee? Which words below do you think describe his artwork? Discuss your answers with your partner.

> abstract   boring   colorful   powerful   realistic   traditional

2 Watch the video. Select (✓) the information we learn about Stan.

☐ Where he's from   ☐ Why he likes painting

☐ His age   ☐ His favorite artist

☐ When he started painting   ☐ What he's interested in

3 Watch the video again. Answer the questions.

1. What is Stan's job?
2. How long has Stan been painting?
3. Why does Stan think it's better to paint on the street than at home?
4. What does Stan say inspires his art?
5. How long did Stan's painting in Bristol take to complete?
6. What will happen to Stan's painting?

4 **GROUP WORK** A street artist is going to paint a new mural in your town. In your group, decide on answers to the questions.

1. Where is the mural going to be painted?
2. What is it going to look like?
3. What message do you want it to express?
4. How do you want people to feel when they see it?

5 **GROUP WORK** Present your idea for the mural to the class. Which other group's idea do you like the best? Why?

Culture Tip

The word *graffiti* comes from the Italian word 'graffio', which means 'scratch'. Art historians think this is because the earliest graffiti was carved on walls.

READING

1 PAIR WORK Look at the title of the article and the photos. What do you think the article is about?

DogVinci

Dogs are smart animals, so they can be trained to do amazing things. They can round up sheep on a farm, act in movies, and guide blind people in the street. And, perhaps surprisingly, some dogs can even paint.

One such dog is Dagger, a black Labrador and golden retriever mix. In his early life, Dagger was training to become an assistance dog for people with disabilities. He was taught how to turn lights on and off, close doors, and hold things in his mouth. Unfortunately, he had some difficulties with feeling frightened and, in the end, had to leave the training program.

Fortunately, he was quickly adopted by New York artist Yvonne Dagger. He spent a lot of time in Yvonne's studio, watching her paint. One summer's day in 2015, Yvonne asked Dagger if he wanted to paint too, and he looked excited. So, she put a brush in his mouth and said "paint"–and he did!

Dagger, or "DogVinci" as he is also lovingly known, has been producing colorful abstract artworks since that day. Yvonne has been selling his paintings and donating some money from each sale to animal-related charities. So far, over 575 paintings have been sold and more than $135,000 has been given to charity. But Dagger has not only been spending his time painting. He's also been working as a therapy dog. He visits schools, libraries, and homes for the elderly and brings comfort and affection to the people there.

Since he started painting, Dagger has become quite famous. He's appeared on many talk shows and news programs. He's also been featured in magazines and newspapers, and a documentary has even been made about him. Journalists, writers, and reporters from as far away as Brazil, the UK, South Korea, and Australia have all wanted to share his amazing story.

2 Read the article. Choose (✓) *True* or *False*.

	True	False
1. Dagger had to stop his training because he got scared.	☐	☐
2. It took a long time to find an owner for Dagger.	☐	☐
3. One day, Dagger picked up a brush and started painting.	☐	☐
4. Dagger has been painting landscapes since 2015.	☐	☐
5. Dagger doesn't always work in Yvonne's studio.	☐	☐
6. Only people in the USA have heard about Dagger's story.	☐	☐

3 PAIR WORK Discuss the questions.

1. If you could meet Yvonne, what questions would you ask about Dagger?
2. What other tasks or activities can dogs be trained to do?
3. In what other ways can animals show creativity?

04 | Who's your best friend?

SPEAKING
Describing people
GRAMMAR
Relative clauses
LISTENING
A high school reunion
READING
Types of friendships

VOCABULARY

WARMUP
Describe your best friend

1 Look at the picture. What are the people like? Write the correct letter. Then listen and check your answers.

a. reserved   b. clumsy   c. organized   d. generous   e. creative   f. talkative

2 Complete the chart with the words in the box. Then add more words from the picture.

charming   insecure   nerdy   outgoing   cautious   optimistic

Departments	Useful characteristics	Less useful characteristics
Product development		
Accounts		
Sales & marketing		

3 PAIR WORK Use the words to describe people you know.

> I don't know anyone who is reserved. Do you?

> Yes. My brother is pretty reserved around new people.

4 PAIR WORK How would you describe yourself? Tell your partner.

> I'm outgoing and talkative.

CONVERSATION

SHE SOUNDS CHARMING.

1:32

1 Complete the conversation. Then watch and check your answers. Practice the conversation with a partner.

    a. jealous   **b.** charming   **c.** in college

Hannah So, look at this, Tom. That's the wedding dress. Isn't it amazing?
Tom Wow! That's beautiful. Do you mind if I ask how it feels to have a new sister-in-law?
Hannah Oh, not at all, Kaiko's like my best friend. We've known each other since we were
    1 _____ . In fact, I was the one who introduced her to my brother.
Tom Really? And how did that go?
Hannah Not so great at first. When they started hanging out together, I was kind of
    2 _____ , but she's the kind of person who you can't stay mad at
    long. She made sure neither of us felt left out.
Tom She must have some great people skills! I can't wait to meet her.
Hannah Oh, you'll love her. Kaiko's **3** _____ .
Tom Cool! Let's get together soon.

2 **PAIR WORK** Practice the conversation again. Use the ideas below. Add your own ideas.

1	2	3
at our old job	insecure	outgoing
in high school	unhappy	optimistic
_____	_____	_____

3 **OVER TO YOU** Work in pairs. Make a video of your conversation. Talk about people in your life.

Student A Describe a person you know. Say where or how you met him / her.
Student B Show interest. Ask what kind of person he / she is.

CONVERSATION TIP

BEING POLITE
When you ask a personal question, first politely ask if it's OK.

Do you mind
if I ask ... ?

Oh, not at all.

LANGUAGE PRACTICE

Relative clauses	Grammar Reference page 117
Subject	**Object**
I was the one **who / that** introduced them. He's the only guy **who / that** can make me laugh. He's that tall man **who / that** bought Joe's car. Those are the books **which / that** helped me.	She's the kind of person **(who / that)** you can't stay mad at for long. She was the first teacher **(who / that)** I had in college. They're neighbors **(who / that)** I've known for years.
Whose	It's a game **(which / that)** we like to play.
That's my friend **whose** son won the contest. She's the one **whose** project got picked.	

1 Complete the sentences with the relative clauses in the box.

> that allows me to be creative   that take you to the parking lot
> ~~who lets me come in late~~   which makes luggage
> whose design won first place   that you see

1. I want a boss ___who lets me come in late___ because I am not a morning person.
2. The stairs _____ are at the end of the hallway.
3. That's the woman _____ , so she received $10,000.
4. I am looking for a job _____ because I have a lot of ideas.
5. I work for a company _____ , so I get good deals on suitcases.

2 PAIR WORK Use relative clauses to complete the sentences about people you know. Then compare answers with a partner. Leave out *who, that,* and *which* when you can.

1. My mom is someone _____ .
2. I have friends _____ .
3. My parents give me advice _____ .
4. My family is full of people _____ .
5. My best friend tells me things _____ .

> My mom is someone who people trust.

> I have friends who are really good at cooking.

PRONUNCIATION *Linking with /w/*

1 Listen. Notice the *w*-linked sounds.

1. Do you know anyone who has a truck?
2. Can you show it to me?
3. How is he?
4. Is this how it goes?

2 Listen again and repeat. Try to link the words.

LISTENING

1 **BEFORE YOU LISTEN** Compare yourself to your best friend. Who is...?

- more outgoing   • nerdier   • more reserved   • more adventurous

2 Listen to people talking about how they met a friend. Number the pictures to match the stories.

A

B

C

3 Listen again. Choose (✓) *True* or *False*.

	True	False
1. Ivy met Jane in the robotics club.	☐	☐
2. Ivy and Jane are insecure about being nerds.	☐	☐
3. Trey and Curtis met at a sports competition.	☐	☐
4. Curtis helped Trey become more outgoing.	☐	☐
5. Beth's mom and dad met in college.	☐	☐
6. Beth's parents fell in love the day they met.	☐	☐

4 **LISTENING PLUS** Listen to two people at their high school reunion. Answer the questions.

1. When did Jane and Louise meet?
2. Who does Jane see in the crowd?
3. How has the person changed?
4. Why does Louise know so much about the person?

5 **GROUP WORK** Discuss these questions.

1. Have you ever had a friend who changed? How did the person change?
2. Are there any old friends you'd like to hear from? Who are they?

> My friend Frances and I used to play soccer together. But then he started playing computer games, and I don't see him much.

SMART TALK   *She's the one who ...* | **Student A:** Turn to page 87.
| **Student B:** Turn to page 99.

READING

1 BEFORE YOU READ Look at the title of the article. What types of friendships do you expect to learn about?

Friendship in the Modern World

If you want to be successful, it helps to have friends. Just ask Larry Page and Sergey Brin. They didn't like each other when they first met at university; in fact, they argued. Later, however, they **reconnected** and started one of the world's best-known companies: Google.

In another example, Leonardo DiCaprio and Kate Winslet met on the set of *Titanic*, one of the most romantic films ever made. While their characters fell in love, the two actors formed a close friendship that has lasted for more than 20 years.

In the tech world, show business, and many other industries, friendships are **vital**. Friends not only help by providing **emotional** and social support, but also share career information and contacts. We need a lot of friends, and we need different kinds, but how can we manage all these social connections?

One answer is to accept that friends form circles around us. The **inner** circle contains our best friends. These are people who know us well because we grew up with them, or we spend a lot of time together. We are **loyal** to this inner circle and would invite them to our wedding. It was reported that DiCaprio walked Winslet down the aisle to her husband when she got married.

Then there is the middle circle. It contains people we see regularly at parties, school, or work **events**. We enjoy conversations about topics that aren't very serious. These friends require less time and energy, yet they can introduce us to new ideas, contacts, or information. We might see them at a wedding, but we wouldn't necessarily invite them to ours.

The third is the **outer** circle. Think of regular customers, friends of friends, and especially social media contacts. We might not remember their names, but they link us to the wider world. These contacts might post photos of their wedding, and we might "like" them.

Of course these circles are **fluid**. Friendships can change depending on time and **circumstances**. However, having different types of friends gives us a stronger network. And who knows, maybe, like Brin and Page, we might meet a person that changes our lives.

2 Read the article. Then choose (✓) the correct column for each of these friendships.

	Inner	Middle	Outer
1. Jim messages a friend's friend to ask about a job at her company.			
2. The Smiths and the Aguilars often go camping together.			
3. Mark and Jess are soccer coaches in the same league.			
4. Dave offers to show the new nurse around the hospital.			

3 PAIR WORK Match each friendship to its benefit.

____ 1. Larry Page and Sergey Brin

____ 2. Kate Winslet and Leonardo DiCaprio

____ 3. Social media friends

a. They share fun photos and videos online.

b. They challenge each other.

c. They have a true lifelong friendship.

4 GROUP WORK Do you agree that there are three types of friendships? How many types of friends or friendships do you have?

WRITING Turn to page 109.

SPEAKING *How did you meet your friend?*

1 Think of a good friend. Complete the chart below.
Add your own question and answer it.

1. When did you meet?	
2. Where did you meet?	
3. Why did you like him / her?	
4. What kind of person is he / she?	
5. What do you like to do together, now?	
6.	

2 PAIR WORK Use your answers to tell a partner about your friend.

> I met Sunny three years ago. We were at a party and neither of us knew anyone, so we started talking.

> Oh really? What did you talk about?

3 PAIR WORK Change partners. Tell your stories again. After you listen to your partner, tell your partner's story to show you understand.

> Let me check I have the story correct: You met ...

4 GROUP WORK Complete the sentences with your own ideas.
Then share them with a group.

1. A best friend is someone who...
2. A best friend is someone who will never...
3. It's good to make friends with people who...
4. (your own sentence) _____

GO ONLINE
for grammar, vocabulary, and speaking practice

5 OVER TO YOU Find an example of a famous friendship. How did the friends meet? What have they done together? Tell a partner.

NOW I CAN

SPEAKING	GRAMMAR	LISTENING	READING
☐ describe what people are like.	☐ use relative clauses.	☐ understand conversations about a high school reunion.	☐ understand types of friendships.

05 | Gotta have it!

SPEAKING
Discussing technology
GRAMMAR
Infinitives and gerunds
LISTENING
Reviews of travel apps
READING
A digital detox

VOCABULARY

WARMUP
How do you use your phone?

1 Look at the picture. What things do you see? Write the correct letter. Then listen and check your answers.

a. game console
b. wireless headphones
c. virtual reality goggles
d. smartphone
e. smartwatch
f. digital assistant
g. tablet
h. sports camera

2 PAIR WORK Answer the questions. Talk about the items in the picture.

1. Which items **don't** you usually leave your home without?
2. Which items are only for entertainment?
3. Which items can talk to you?

3 PAIR WORK Ask and answer questions using technology words.

Do you have a smartwatch?

Yes, I do. It helps me stay fit.

VOCABULARY TIP

To remember nouns, think of pictures for the words you want to learn. For example, imagine people wearing virtual reality goggles.

CONVERSATION

HOW CAN I LIVE WITHOUT IT?

1:32

▶1 Complete the conversation. Then watch and check your answers. Practice the conversation with a partner.

a. not possible	b. giving up your phone	c. check my messages	d. a meeting

Ricardo Hey, Scott. What are you looking for?

Scott My phone. I can't find it, and I'm late for **1**_____.

Ricardo Try looking in your car.

Scott I did, and it's not there!

Ricardo Do you have to have it? Why don't you just go without it?

Scott Are you kidding? I need it to **2**_____.

Ricardo You can manage for a day, can't you?

Scott No, I can't. My phone is like part of my brain!

Ricardo That seems kind of scary. I think you should try **3**_____ for a day.

Scott That's **4**_____. People need to be able to reach me in case there is an emergency.

Ricardo The world won't end, Scott. I forgot to wear my smartwatch to work last Friday, and I managed to go all day without thinking about it!

◯2 **PAIR WORK** Practice the conversation again. Use the ideas below. Add your own ideas.

1	2	3	4
an appointment	find places	going phone free	unrealistic
a class	contact people	turning it off	difficult
_____	_____	_____	_____

◉3 **OVER TO YOU** Work in pairs. Make a video of your conversation. Talk about technology.

Student A Explain how you use your phone. Say if you could live without it for a day.

Student B Give your opinion.

LANGUAGE PRACTICE

Infinitives and gerunds
Grammar Reference page 118

Infinitives

I need it **to check** my messages.

I use it **to pay** bills.

Gerunds

I need it for **checking** my messages.

I use it for **paying** bills.

Try **looking** in your car.

Infinitive phrases

I use a meditation app **(in order) to relax** before bed.

I need her contact info **(in order) to send** the link.

(In order) to send the image, your phone will need a wireless connection.

1 Choose the correct phrase to complete the sentence.

1. She went online (to improve)/ for improve her English.

2. This software is good **for protect / for protecting** your computer against viruses.

3. My daughter hides her phone under her pillow in order **to chat / for chat** with her friends.

4. There's a great new app **for practice / for practicing** vocabulary.

2 Rewrite the conversations using gerunds.

1. A What do you use your phone for the most?

   B I use my phone to play games. _____ .

2. A How do you use your sports camera?

   B I use my sports camera to record my motorcycle rides. _____ .

3. A What do you need your tablet for?

   B I need my tablet to read comic books. _____ .

4. A What other technology do you use every day?

   B I use my digital assistant to listen to podcasts. _____ .

3 **PAIR WORK** Give your own responses to the questions in activity 2. Then practice the conversation with a partner.

> What do you use your phone for the most?

> I use it for playing games!

PRONUNCIATION *Reduction of* have got to

1 Listen. Notice the reduced sound of *have got to*.

Unreduced	Reduced
1. I've got to have it.	I /gatə/ have it.
2. I've got to charge my phone.	I /gatə/ charge my phone.
3. They've got to leave soon.	They /gatə/ leave soon.
4. You've got to see this video.	You /gatə/ see this video.

2 Listen again and repeat. Try to say the reduced forms.

LISTENING

1 **BEFORE YOU LISTEN** Discuss these questions with a partner.

1. What travel apps have you **downloaded**?
2. How do you **browse** for information when you travel?
3. What **features** would you expect to see in a travel app?

2 Listen to reviews of apps. Number the apps in the order you hear about them.

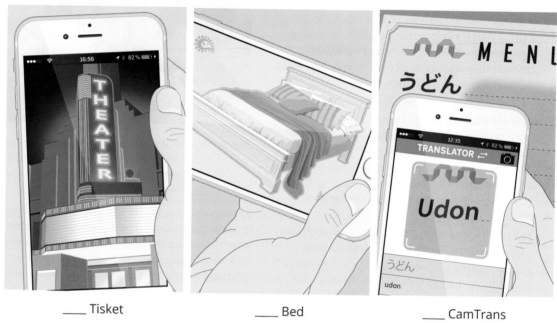

_____ Tisket   _____ Bed   _____ CamTrans

3 Listen again. Choose (✓) the app that fits the description. More than one app may be possible.

	Bed	CamTrans	Tisket	
1.				is convenient for international travel.
2.				is good for finding an unusual hotel.
3.				helps people who read and write in different languages.
4.				offers cheap tickets for shows and concerts.
5.				is free.
6.				costs ten dollars.

4 **LISTENING PLUS** Listen to the callers. Use the phrases in the box to complete the sentences.

App	Feature
Local Buddy	share information about life in a motor home
Wandering	keep all your travel plans organized in one place
Tripper	connect travelers with friendly local people

1. Ella recommends _____ . It helps you _____ .
2. Raj likes _____ It can _____ .
3. Barbara and her husband designed _____ so people can _____ .

SMART TALK *Apps for active people* | **Student A:** Turn to page 88.
Student B: Turn to page 100.

READING

1 **BEFORE YOU READ** How many times a day do you look at your phone?

Is it Time for a **Digital Detox?**

by Liz Morgan

Have you ever gone to your phone to check a text and then lost an hour of your time to social media? That is meant to happen. Tech companies have employed a great many **psychologists** because they want to attract you to your handheld **device** . . . and keep you there.

Here's how it works. When you hear the ping of a **notification** on your phone or computer, your brain **releases** a special **chemical** called dopamine. It causes you to feel **pleasure**—someone is contacting you! You check, and once you are on your phone, it's hard to get off. You might start checking for other messages to keep the dopamine coming.

The result is that spending a lot of time on screens may bring a little happiness, but it also makes you want more: the average person touches their phone more than 2000 times a day. Habits and **impulses** can become **addictions**. This happens when work, school, or relationships suffer because a person cannot stop the behavior. For example, a college student might fail a course because they spend too much time playing video games.

Experts say that if you recognize that your device is taking up too much time, it might be time for a digital detox. This means going offline for a few days or even a week. If this seems impossible, you might need some help.

In one study, a group of adults were invited to a device-free vacation. Scientists who were secretly **observing** them noted big changes in their behavior over four days. The people became more social, they sat up straighter, and paid more attention to each other in conversation. These people slept better. They also made long-term plans to improve their lives.

Studies, such as this one, suggest that there are benefits to being offline for a period of time, and that it can have positive effects on your mental health.

2 Read the article. Choose (✓) *True, False,* or *Not given.*

	True	False	Not given
1. The technology industry works hard to get people to spend time on their devices.	☐	☐	☐
2. A typical person might message 200 people in a day.	☐	☐	☐
3. It is impossible to be addicted to technology.	☐	☐	☐
4. Taking a break from technology is called a digital detox.	☐	☐	☐

3 Read the article again. Choose the answer with the correct order according to the article.

1. **a.** You get a message. You feel pleasure. Your brain releases dopamine.

   b. You get a message. Your brain releases dopamine. You feel pleasure.

2. **a.** A person spends a lot of time online. He stops sleeping. He gets in trouble at work.

   b. A person gets in trouble at work. He stops sleeping. He spends a lot of time online.

3. **a.** People get to know each other. They go on vacation. They turn off their phones.

   b. People turn off their phones. They go on vacation. They get to know each other better.

4 **GROUP WORK** Discuss these questions.

1. What do you feel about the amount of time you spend on screens? Explain.

2. Would you ever try a digital detox? Explain.

 WRITING Turn to page 110.

SPEAKING How do you use technology?

1 Think about how you use technology. Complete the chart. Add your own question.

Do you use technology for ...

	Not much	Sometimes	A lot
making and sharing content?			
watching movies and videos?			
playing games?			
learning new skills and information?			
texting or calling friends and family?			
shopping?			
_____			

2 **CLASS ACTIVITY** Walk around the room. Ask questions from the chart and survey your classmates.

> Do you use technology for making content?

> No, not much. I post a few photos is all.

> Actually, yes, you should check out my videos!

3 **GROUP WORK** In groups of four, share your survey results. Then discuss these questions.

1. Which technology activities are the most popular in your class?
2. Which technology activities are the easiest to give up?

4 **CLASS ACTIVITY** Share your answers. Does technology make you more or less social and / or creative? Do the results surprise you?

5 **OVER TO YOU** Look for a chart or graph that gives information about how people use mobile devices. Share your information with the class.

GO ONLINE
for grammar, vocabulary, and speaking practice

NOW I CAN

SPEAKING
☐ talk about technology.

GRAMMAR
☐ use infinitives and gerunds.

LISTENING
☐ understand reviews of travel apps.

READING
☐ understand how a digital detox works.

06 | He'd never seen the desert.

SPEAKING
Describing events

GRAMMAR
Past perfect

LISTENING
A fictional travel story

READING
An online house rental

WARMUP
Where did you go on your last vacation?

VOCABULARY

 1 Look at the picture. How would you describe the people? Write the correct letter. Then listen and check your answers.

| **a.** angry | **b.** in a hurry | **c.** noisy | **d.** patient | **e.** cheerful | **f.** careless |

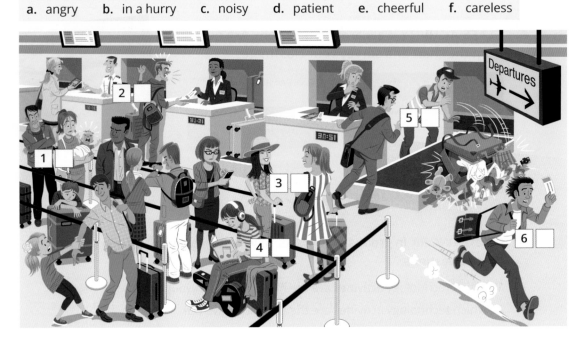

2 Look at the picture again. Complete the sentences with phrases in the box to describe these people.

| reluctant to say goodbye | anxious about her baby | enthusiastic about music | late for a flight |

1. Marco is running to the gate. He's _____ .
2. Sarah loves pop songs. She's _____ .
3. Laura doesn't want her father to go. She's _____ .
4. Little Mikey cries a lot. His mother is _____ .

3 PAIR WORK Describe other people in the picture. How do they feel?

4 PAIR WORK Describe your experiences traveling. Use the words and phrases from activities 1 and 2.

> I was enthusiastic about flying, but my sister was reluctant to get on the plane.

CONVERSATION

HOW WAS YOUR TRIP?

1:32

1 Complete the conversation. Then watch and check your answers. Practice the conversation with a partner.

a. museums   b. friend   c. mechanical problems

Hannah	Tom! You're back! How was your trip to Brazil?
Tom	Great, once I got there. My flight was delayed by **1** _____ . By the time my plane finally landed in Rio, my connecting flight had left.
Hannah	Oh, I hate it when that happens!
Tom	I know. Luckily, I have a **2** _____ who lives in Rio, so I decided to stay there for a few days.
Hannah	Was he surprised to hear from you?
Tom	Yes, and it turned out great. I hadn't met his family, so we all spent some time together. Rio's great!
Hannah	I bet! I've never been, but I'd love to go. Did you go to any **3** _____ ?
Tom	Well, the kids were pretty young, so we went to the beach.
Hannah	Good for you! Rio's got the best beaches in the world!

2 PAIR WORK Practice the conversation again. Use the ideas below. Add your own ideas.

1	2	3
the weather	cousin	sights
runway traffic	uncle	concerts
_____	_____	_____

3 OVER TO YOU Work in pairs. Make a video of your conversation. Talk about a recent travel experience.

Student A   Talk about a trip. Say what you did and didn't enjoy.
Student B   Show interest and ask for more information.

CONVERSATION TIP

EXPRESSING EMOTION
Show you are interested by reacting to what someone says.

... my connecting flight had left.

Oh, I hate it when that happens!

LANGUAGE PRACTICE

Past perfect	Grammar Reference page 119
Simple past	**Past perfect**
By the time my plane landed in Rio,	my connecting flight **had left.**
When we got to the station,	the train **had** just **arrived.**
They couldn't get home	because she **had lost** her passport.
Past perfect	**Simple past**
I **hadn't been** there before,	so I took a bike tour of the city.
How long **had** you **studied** French	before you went to Paris?

1 Complete the sentences. Use the simple past or the past perfect.

1. By the time he ____arrived____ (arrive) at the airport, his plane ____had left____ (leave).

2. They _____ (visit) the aquarium, so we _____ (go) shopping.

3. I _____ (live) here a while before I _____ (feel) comfortable
   with the language.

4. She _____ (not get lost) when her phone died because she _____ (bring)
   a map.

5. They _____ (travel) to Europe many times, so they _____ (decide)
   to go to Asia this year.

6. When Mary _____ (call) for a taxi, we _____ (just / finish) packing.

2 PAIR WORK Talk about the events in each sentence in activity 1. Which event
happened first?

> First, his plane left. Then he arrived at the airport.

3 PAIR WORK Ask and answer the questions. Use the past perfect where appropriate.

1. Where did you go on your last vacation? Had you been there before?

2. Who did you travel with? Had you traveled with that person before?

3. What did you do there? Had you ever done that before?

4. What had you expected the place to be like? What was different?

> My cousin and I went to Cancún last year. I'd been ...

PRONUNCIATION *Reduction of* had *in the past perfect*

1 Listen. Notice the reduced sound of the helping verb *had.*

Unreduced	Reduced
1. The flight had already left.	The /flaɪtəd/ already left.
2. Pam had packed a sweater.	/pæməd/ packed a sweater.
3. How long had you been there?	How /lɔŋəd/ you been there?
4. What had you expected to see?	/wʌtəd/ you expected to see?

2 Listen again and repeat. Try to say the reduced forms.

LISTENING

1 **BEFORE YOU LISTEN** Write the letter of the description next to the matching audiobook cover.

a.

By Mina Lynsky
Dancing with Dracula

This fascinating travel guide explores the history of folk dance in Eastern Europe.

1. ____

b.

By Therese Fortune
Women of the Island

Listeners will enjoy this collection of stories set at the fictional Tradewinds Hotel where people can connect in unexpected ways.

2. ____

c.

By Ray Spring
Three Nights in the Desert

A newly married couple get their dream job filming a travel series about California's Death Valley, but the desert can be a dangerous place ...

3. ____

2 Listen. Number the sentences in chronological order. Which audiobook in activity 1 is it?

a. ____ They see something shining on a hill.

b. ____ The stars come out.

c. ____ They run out of water.

d. ____ Their car breaks down.

e. ____ A truck passes them on the highway.

3 Listen again. Answer the questions.

1. Who knows more about cars?

2. Who does not want to look for water?

3. Who makes a wish?

4. Who notices the light on a hill?

4 **LISTENING PLUS** Listen to chapter 10. Choose (✓) *True*, *False*, or *Not given*.

	True	False	Not given
1. Liam wants to stay near the car.	☐	☐	☐
2. Cici is afraid of snakes.	☐	☐	☐
3. The couple use the light of the moon to see.	☐	☐	☐
4. They meet a group of dangerous criminals.	☐	☐	☐

5 **GROUP WORK** Work together to decide on an ending for the chapter. Then share your story with the class.

I have an idea! The husband disappears in the night.

Maybe a snake bites him.

SMART TALK *By the time she was 18, ...*

Student A: Turn to page 89.
Student B: Turn to page 101.

READING

1 BEFORE YOU READ Look at the photo and the text. What type of text is it?

a. a real estate ad   b. an online travel magazine   c. a home rental site for travelers

Available Homes 🏠 🛏

Beautiful Beach House

Come and enjoy a tropical island **paradise** on the island of Key Largo in the Florida Keys! Our two-bedroom, one bath beach house is in a private community just minutes from the ocean. You'll enjoy **access** to private beaches as well as an enormous swimming pool with a play area for the kids. There is shopping and **fine dining** nearby as well as boat rentals and other activities.

This **cozy** little home can sleep up to six people. It has a full kitchen, outdoor grill, air conditioning, and free wifi. The first bedroom has a king-sized bed. Bedroom two has a queen, and there is a fold out couch for the kids.

Reviews ⭐⭐⭐⭐✩ (415) reviews

⭐⭐⭐⭐✩   **Stayed in January**

Carmela

This was our third trip to the Florida Keys. We love island life, and our stay at this cottage was pleasant. The home was clean and the hosts had provided everything we needed. The only **downside** was discovering that the "short walk" to the beach was not so short. It took us 20 minutes!

Host's response: We are glad you enjoyed the cottage. We will update our description of the neighborhood!

⭐⭐⭐⭐⭐   **Stayed in March**

Maryam

My husband and I were **delighted** with this cute little beach house we had found for our family vacation. But we also discovered the kindness of our hosts Alvin and Betsy who helped us get through a medical emergency. We had spent a fun day with the grandkids at the pool, and we were getting ready for bed when George started having chest pains. Our daughter and son-in-law had gone out to dinner, so we called Alvin who came straight over. Betsy stayed with the kids and Alvin drove us to the hospital. His fast thinking saved George's life. We think they **deserve** far more than a 5-star review, so we are giving them 10 stars!

Host's response: Maryam, we were happy to help, and we are so glad that George is better!

 2 Read the text. Answer the questions.

1. Where is the home?
2. How many guests can stay there?
3. What can guests do at the cottage?
4. What can guests do in the community?
5. What might make people reluctant to stay at the house?
6. What might make people happy about staying there?

3 PAIR WORK If you could bring six people to this vacation rental for a holiday weekend, who would you bring? How would you spend your three days?

WRITING Turn to page 110.

SPEAKING *My travel nightmare*

1 **PAIR WORK** Match the travel disaster to the picture. Then discuss which situation is the worst.

1 ☐ 2 ☐ 3 ☐

a. We couldn't find the hotel because my phone had died.

b. I had forgotten my wallet, so I couldn't go on the tour.

c. Suddenly, I realized I had eaten something bad, and I had to leave the table.

2 Use the information in the charts and your own ideas to make true or false stories about yourself.

When I got to the	beach hotel	I realized that I had forgotten to bring my	swimsuit. sun block.
I was walking in	Tokyo Rio de Janeiro	when I discovered that I had gotten lost.	
I had started feeling	sick hungry	so I decided to	leave early. go back to the hotel.
_____	_____	_____	_____

3 **PAIR WORK** Tell your travel stories. Your partner must guess true or false.

> I was walking in Mexico City when I fell and broke my wrist. A nice lady helped me find a taxi to get to a hospital.

> I think that's true!

> No, it's actually a false story. I went to Mexico City, but I didn't fall.

4 **CLASS ACTIVITY** Think of a new travel story with your partner. Then tell it to the class. The class votes to guess if the story is true or false.

5 **OVER TO YOU** Find photos of a place you want to travel. Talk about activities you would like to do there to the class.

GO ONLINE
for grammar, vocabulary, and speaking practice

NOW I CAN

SPEAKING	GRAMMAR	LISTENING	READING
☐ describe events in the past.	☐ use the past perfect.	☐ understand a fictional travel story.	☐ understand an online house rental.

VIDEO

1:32
Can a computer write a musical?

1 **PAIR WORK** Look at the pictures. What makes a good musical theater show? How is technology used in theater shows? Discuss your answers with your partner.

2 Watch the video. Match the people to their role.

____ 1. Benjamin, Nathan, Neil, Luke
____ 2. Pablo
____ 3. Alex, James
____ 4. Nick

a. collecting data
b. creating music by computer
c. creating lyrics by computer
d. creating musicals

3 Watch the video again. Complete the sentences with ONE word.

1. Musicals need to have enjoyable songs and _____ music.

2. Benjamin and Nathan go to a _____ to find out what makes a good story.

3. Audiences like stories with a happy _____ .

4. The story is about a _____ and a child.

5. The software which creates the lyrics starts by showing single _____ .

6. Benjamin and Nick are _____ about finding good music in time.

7. The experiment shows that with imagination and hard _____ , anything is possible.

4 **PAIR WORK** Discuss the questions.

1. Would you be interested in seeing the musical shown in the video? Why / why not?

2. What do you think computers can do as well as or better than people can?

> ### Culture Tip
>
> The West End is London's main theater district, where the first theater opened in 1663. The longest-running show, *The Mousetrap*, has been performed continuously since 1952. The longest-running musical, *Les Misérables*, opened in 1985.

READING

1 Look at the email. Who is the person writing to? Why is she writing?

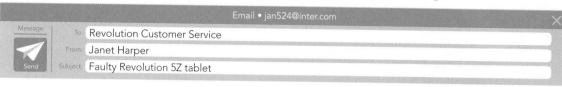

Email • jan524@inter.com

Message	To:	Revolution Customer Service
	From:	Janet Harper
	Subject:	Faulty Revolution 5Z tablet

Dear Sir or Madam:

I am writing to complain about a Revolution 5Z tablet that I bought at your Richmond store on September 21.

Before buying the device, I had read many reviews online which had rated it very highly. I wanted a simple tablet which I could use for browsing the web and sending emails. The Revolution 5Z sounded perfect. I am, however, cautious about shopping online, so I decided to visit your store. I was served by a charming salesperson, who patiently answered all my questions. After I had spoken to him, I felt even more enthusiastic and decided to buy the tablet.

When I got home, I charged the battery fully, as I had been told to do. After I had done this, I turned it on and it became clear there was a problem, as there were wavy lines across the screen. I therefore returned to the store the next day to explain the issue. This time, I spoke to a different salesperson who was not very cheerful and actually seemed reluctant to help. I think perhaps he was in a hurry to go for his lunch break. Anyway, in the end, I left the tablet with him to be repaired. He said it would be ready a week later. However, that was over two weeks ago. I've tried phoning the store a couple of times, but nobody seems to know when I'll get my tablet back.

I am very disappointed, not only with the faulty product, but with the terrible service that I have received. I would therefore like to request a full refund if I do not receive the repaired tablet by the end of this week.

Sincerely,

Janet Harper

2 Read the email. Choose the correct answers to complete the sentences.

1. Janet wanted a tablet she could use for ...

   a. sending emails   **b.** using the Internet   **c.** sending emails and using the Internet

2. Janet was happy with the service from ...

   a. the first salesperson   **b.** the second salesperson   **c.** both salespeople

3. There was a problem with the tablet's ...

   a. battery   **b.** screen   **c.** battery and screen

4. Janet visited the store on ...

   a. September 21   **b.** September 22   **c.** September 21 and 22

5. Janet has ... the store a few times but nobody can help her.

   a. called   **b.** emailed   **c.** called and emailed

6. Janet is unhappy with ...

   a. the service   **b.** the tablet   **c.** the service and the tablet

3 GROUP WORK Have you ever bought something which didn't work properly? What did you do about it? Tell your group.

> I once bought some wireless headphones which stopped working after a few weeks. I took them back to the store and they exchanged them for another pair.

07 | Time for a new look!

SPEAKING
Describing appearances
GRAMMAR
Have / get something done
LISTENING
A new look
READING
A double makeover

WARMUP
Where do you go
for a haircut?

VOCABULARY

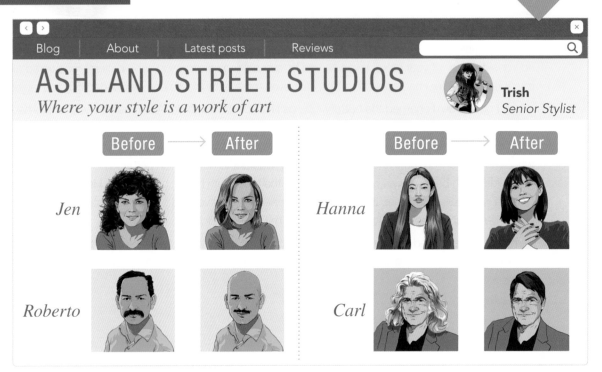

Blog | About | Latest posts | Reviews

ASHLAND STREET STUDIOS
Where your style is a work of art

Trish
Senior Stylist

Before → After   Before → After

Jen   Hanna

Roberto   Carl

1 Look at the pictures. What did the hair stylist do to her customers? Complete the sentences with the words in the box. Then listen and check your answers.

| highlights | pierced | shaved | dyed x2 | cut | manicure | straightened | trimmed |

1. Trish <u>straightened</u> Jen's hair and gave her _____ . She also _____ Jen's ears.
2. Trish _____ Roberto's head and _____ his mustache.
3. Trish _____ Hanna's hair blue and gave her a _____ .
4. Trish _____ Carl's hair and _____ it brown.

2 **PAIR WORK** Have you ever done any of these things? Compare your answers.

> Have you ever dyed your hair?

> No, never. Have you?

3 **PAIR WORK** What are some things you want to try for a new look? Tell your partner.

A I want to straighten my hair and dye it pink!

B I think that would look good on you!

VOCABULARY TIP

Think of personal stories to remember new words.

My little sister trimmed my hair, and now I'm wearing a hat to work.

44

CONVERSATION

I'VE HAD A HAIRCUT.

1:32

▶1 Complete the conversation. Then watch and check your answers. Practice the conversation with a partner.

a. an interview   **b.** highlights   **c.** model   **d.** downtown

Lily   Patrick! I almost didn't recognize you!
Patrick   Hi, Lily. It's good to see you!
Lily   You look great! Are you going to **1** _____ ?
Patrick   No, just lunch with a friend.
Lily   Well, you seem different.
Patrick   I hope so! Now that I have a real job, I thought I should buy a suit, and get my hair cut. I went to that new place **2** _____ . Do you like it?
Lily   Oh yeah! I didn't know you had such great taste.
Patrick   Well, my friend Alex has been helping me out. You know Alex. You met him at the restaurant last week.
Lily   Oh, that Alex. He's a **3** _____ , isn't he?
Patrick   Not exactly. He works in fashion, though, and he says this suit will be good for my career.
Lily   It probably will be! So, what else are you doing?
Patrick   Well, for the first time in my life, I'm going to get **4** _____ .

◯2 **PAIR WORK** Practice the conversation again. Use the ideas below. Add your own ideas.

1	2	3	4
a party	at the mall	stylist	a manicure
a wedding	near my office	fashion designer	a barbershop shave
_____	_____	_____	_____

◯3 **OVER TO YOU** Work in pairs. Make a video of your conversation. Talk about your appearance.

Student A   Give your partner a compliment about their appearance.
Student B   Accept the praise and tell the story about it.

LANGUAGE PRACTICE

Have / *get* something done	Grammar Reference page 120
Active	**Causative**
I cut my hair.	I **had** / **got** my hair **cut**.
(I cut it *myself*.)	(*Someone else* cut it.)
I'm going to cut my hair.	I'm going to **have** / **get** my hair **cut**.
(*I'm* going to cut it.)	(*Someone else* is going to cut it.)
How often does he trim his beard?	Did you **get** your ears **pierced**?
He trims it every week.	Yes, I **got** them **pierced** yesterday.
Why did she do her nails?	What do you want to **have done**?
She did them for the party.	I want to **have** my hair **dyed**.

1 Put the words in the correct order to make sentences.
Are the sentences active or causative?

1. my / done/ nails / going / I'm / get / to ____I'm going to get my nails done. = causative____

2. didn't / He / want / blue / hair / have / his / dyed / to _____ .

3. He / his / trimmed / got / beard _____ .

4. shave / to / his / going / head / He's _____ .

5. pierced / get / to / She / wants / ears / her _____ .

6. When / straighten / you / your / hair / did _____ ?

2 **PAIR WORK** Rewrite the conversation using causative sentences.
Then practice it with a partner.

A Where are you going?

B To that new salon. *I need to cut my hair.* _____ .

A Really? But it looks fine now.

B Thanks, but I need a change. *I'm going to dye it, too.* _____ .

A But it looks great the way it is!

B No, it's too curly. *I want to straighten it as well.* _____ .

A Wow! That's a completely new look!

B I know, but that's what *I want to do!* _____ .

PRONUNCIATION   *Reduced vowel /ə/ (schwa)*

1 Listen. Notice the reduced sound of certain vowels in words with more than one syllable.

1. interesting /ˈɪntrəstɪŋ/

2. straightened /ˈstreɪtənd/

3. manicure /ˈmænəkyʊr/

4. tonight /təˈnaɪt/

5. cousin /ˈkʌzən/

6. appearance /ˈəpɪrəns/

2 Listen again and repeat. Try to say the /ə/ sound.

LISTENING

1 **BEFORE YOU LISTEN** Match the descriptions to the pictures.

a. Grace has started wearing scarves, belts, and other **accessories** for a more **polished** appearance.

b. Mavis loves her **curly** hair and casual wardrobe.

c. Nora was tired of her hair, so she got a **blow out** to straighten it.

2 Listen to the conversation. What does Stella have done at the salon? Select (✓) the correct answers.

☐ 1. a new color   ☐ 4. highlights

☐ 2. a haircut   ☐ 5. a manicure

☐ 3. a blow out

3 Listen again. Choose the best description.

1. Stella wants to look like …

    a. an organized professional.

    b. a fashionable person.

2. Eileen's advice for Stella is to straighten her hair so it lasts for

    a. a year.

    b. a day or two.

3. Stella and Eileen …

    a. have a good client-customer relationship.

    b. disagree about how to achieve Stella's goals.

4 **LISTENING PLUS** Listen to the outcome. Complete the sentences with words from the box.

| straight | curly | presentation | professional | surprised | satisfied |

1. Stella came in with _____ hair and left with _____ hair.

2. Eileen helped Stella feel ready for her _____ by giving her a _____ hair style.

3. Stella was _____ when she first saw the change but she was _____ in the end.

5 **GROUP WORK** Discuss these questions.

1. Would you trust a hair stylist to change your look before an important event? Explain.

2. What is the most dramatic change you have made to your appearance? Tell your story.

SMART TALK *Before and after* | Student A: Turn to page 90. Student B: Turn to page 102. | 47

READING

1 **BEFORE YOU READ** Look at the picture and the description of the blog. Who do you think the double makeover is for?

Blog | About | Latest posts | Archives

Married in Manhattan
A blog about living in the city by Rachel and Jed

A Double Makeover?

Would you let your **spouse** dress you for a week? It's a test of true love and it requires having **faith** that the person you married wants you to look your best. But why take a chance?

Apparently, everyone else is doing it! That's what my husband Jed says. He works in the fashion industry, and having your partner dress you is a way to rethink your **wardrobe**. So we decided to give it a go.

Day one was a workday. I started with Jed's favorite **plaid** shirt. I paired it with blue jeans and ankle-high boots, and to accessorize, I added a red scarf and some mirrored sunglasses. Jed nodded. He was going to have lunch with friends, and he said it was just the right amount of casual.

When it was my turn, Jed pulled a brown leather skirt from the back of my closet and matched it with a navy and white blouse. I was surprised by the combination, but I liked the effect. I went off to a business meeting feeling more interesting than usual.

Next, we decided to try dressing each other for a party downtown. That upped the challenge because Jed's fashion friends would be there. Nervously, I opened his closet, closed my eyes, and picked a shirt. It was pink. I paired it with black jeans and a green jacket. Jed raised his eyebrows. I quickly exchanged the jacket for a more **subtle** gray one.

Then Jed surprised me with a dress from one of his fashion shoots. It was a beautiful deep turquoise with a **loose** flowing skirt. I liked his choice for jewelry: a colorful beaded necklace. I felt **chic** and comfortable. But Jed looked at me with a critical eye.

"You would look fantastic with red hair," he said.

"I'll do it if you get your beard shaved off," I responded.

So we went to a salon, and I got my hair dyed bright red, and Jed got his beard shaved off. Pleased, we walked all the way downtown to the party. We had a great time, and I realized that interesting clothes start conversations. The experiment was a success, so we may do it again next week!

2 Read the blog. How successful was the makeover experiment? Explain.

3 Read the blog again. Choose (✓) *True* or *False*.

	True	False
1. It is becoming popular for couples to dress each other.	☐	☐
2. Jed was happy to wear informal clothes to a lunch date.	☐	☐
3. Rachel did not expect the outfit Jed chose for her business meeting.	☐	☐
4. Jed got his beard trimmed.	☐	☐
5. Rachel's hair is a natural red.	☐	☐

4 **GROUP WORK** Discuss these questions.

1. Have you ever helped or would you ever help someone else choose an outfit? Explain your answer.
2. What does the way you dress say about you? What are some examples?

WRITING Turn to page 111.

SPEAKING *A makeover?*

1 These people are making changes to their lives. What should they get done? Choose one person and complete the chart.

Mia Logan, 22

new college graduate

starting a career in a bank

sings in a pop music band at night

loves bright colors

doesn't like spending money on her appearance

Kurt Jacobs, 27

professional video gamer

meeting his girlfriend's wealthy family

has a big presence on social media

travels frequently

has a part-time job at a gym

	A makeover for ... Mia ☐		Kurt ☐	
hair	clothes	shoes	accessories	other
get her hair cut				

2 **GROUP WORK** Make a group with people who chose the same person. Discuss your suggestions in the chart. Give reasons.

> Mia should get her hair cut and dyed.

> Do you really think so? I was wondering if she could just get it trimmed.

3 **PAIR WORK** Find a partner who chose the other person. Compare your answers. Do you agree with your partner's ideas?

4 **OVER TO YOU** Find a photo of a look you like. Tell a classmate what the look says about the person's personality and lifestyle.

GO ONLINE for grammar, vocabulary, and speaking practice

NOW I CAN

SPEAKING
☐ describe people's appearances.

GRAMMAR
☐ use *have / get* something done.

LISTENING
☐ understand conversations about a new look.

READING
☐ understand a makeover story.

08 | My life would be great!

SPEAKING
Describing places
GRAMMAR
Second conditional
LISTENING
Town hall meeting
READING
Intergenerational schools

WARMUP
What do you like about your neighborhood?

VOCABULARY

1 Look at the photos. What do you see? Write the correct letter.
Then listen and check your answers.

a. vehicle traffic   c. bike lanes   e. pedestrians
b. art scene   d. nightlife   f. public transportation

1

2

3

4

5

6

2 The following affect where people choose to live. Which are important for each group?
Complete the chart with phrases in the box. Add more words from the photos.

| crime rate | public parks | housing prices | shops and restaurants |
| job opportunities | school system | cost of living | air quality |

Single people in their 20s	Families with young children	Retired people

3 **PAIR WORK** Ask and answer questions about where you live.

How are the public parks where you live?

Not bad. There's one park my family and I go to most weekends for a cookout.

50

CONVERSATION

IT'S A GREAT NEIGHBORHOOD.

◼️ 1:32

 1 Complete the conversation. Then watch and check your answers. Practice the conversation with a partner.

   a. French   **b.** bus stop   **c.** nightlife

Amy   So how do you like life in the big city? Is your new apartment working out?

Ricardo   Well, if it were a little bigger, my life would be perfect, but the location is fantastic. This area has great **1**   .

Amy   Cool! I can't wait to visit! And how do you get around?

Ricardo   There's a **2**   around the corner from my apartment.

Amy   Not bad! So you don't need a car?

Ricardo   No, I don't. If I had a car, I'd have to pay a lot of money for parking. As it is, I can walk to most places, and there are some excellent restaurants around here. In fact, there's an amazing **3**   place around the corner.

Amy   Sounds like you're spending a lot of money on food!

Ricardo   I try not to eat out too much, but there aren't many places for me to shop for groceries, so I have an excuse!

Amy   That reminds me. I need to pick up some food for dinner. I've got to run, but I'm glad we got a chance to catch up. If I didn't live so far away, I'd come over for coffee!

 2 **PAIR WORK** Practice the conversation again. Use the ideas below. Add your own ideas.

1	2	3
shops	train station	pizza
public parks	subway stop	Indian
_____	_____	_____

 3 **OVER TO YOU** Work in pairs. Make a video of your conversation. Talk about where you live.

Student A   Talk about what you like and dislike about your home and neighborhood.

Student B   Respond. Then change the subject.

CONVERSATION TIP

MAKING CONNECTIONS
When you want to change the subject, refer to something the other person just said.

> I try not to eat out too much ...

> That reminds me. I need to pick up some food for dinner.

LANGUAGE PRACTICE

> **Second conditional**   Grammar Reference page 121
>
> **If** it were a little bigger, my life **would** be perfect.
> **If** I **had** a cheaper place, I **wouldn't** worry about money.
> **If** the subway **were** closer, you **could** sleep in later!
> **If** I **lived** here, I **might** eat out every night.
> It **would** be great **if** we had air-conditioning.
> What **would** you do **if** you **were** the mayor?
>   **If** I **were** the mayor, I **would** build a new hospital.
> NOTE: I would → I'd

1   Complete the sentences. Use the correct form of the verbs in parentheses.

1. If I _____ had _____ (have) the money, I __ would open __ (open) a coffee shop around here.

2. I _____ (not complain) about our town if the schools _____ (be) better.

3. More tourists _____ (visit) here if the crime rate _____ (not be) so high.

4. If there _____ (not be) so much traffic, I _____ (not be) so stressed out!

5. If I _____ (be) the mayor, I _____ (build) more public parks.

2   Complete the sentences with *would, wouldn't, could,* or *might*.

1. If I were rich, I _____ spend the money on myself. I'd donate it to charity.

2. My life _____ definitely be great if I didn't have to work.

3. If I were the mayor, I _____ spend money on public transportation, but I'm not sure.

4. If the cost of living were lower, I _____ afford to go shopping more.

5. If I had a big house, I _____ have more parties.

3   **PAIR WORK** Tell your partner your own answers for the situations in activity 2.

> If I were rich, I might buy my own private island!

> I would travel all over the world!

PRONUNCIATION *Reduction of* would you

1   Listen. Notice the reduced sound of *would you*.

Unreduced	Reduced
1. If it were closer, would you walk there?	If it were closer, /wədʒə/ walk there?
2. If you were in charge, what would you do?	If you were in charge, what /wədʒə/ do?
3. If you had the money, would you buy me that?	If you had the money, /wədʒə/ buy me that?

2   Listen again and repeat. Try to say the reduced form.

LISTENING

1 BEFORE YOU LISTEN **Look at the photo. Write the correct letter.**

a. protected bicycle lanes   c. vehicle lanes

b. designated bus lanes   d. pedestrian-friendly sidewalks

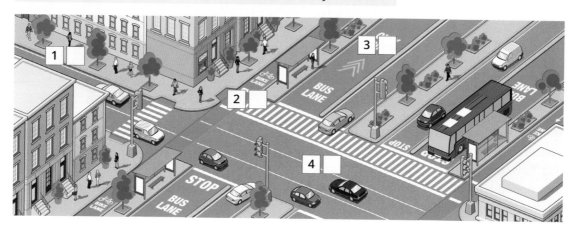

2 **Listen to the town hall meeting. Choose (✓) the correct statements.**

☐ 1. Marshall Street will be closed to cars.

☐ 2. Bicycle riders will be safer.

☐ 3. There will be special lanes only for buses.

☐ 4. Pedestrians will have more space to walk.

☐ 5. Business owners on Marshall Street approve of the plan.

3 **Listen again. How do the different people feel about the plan? Match the statement to the speaker.**

____ 1. Alan   a. I'm worried that there will be more traffic problems on Marshall Street.

____ 2. Paula   b. I like the idea of having a safer journey to school.

____ 3. Mike   c. I'm proud of this plan, and I think it will make life better for everyone.

____ 4. Rosie   d. My neighbors will be excited about the changes to Marshall Street.

4 LISTENING PLUS **Listen to the rest of the meeting and answer the questions.**

1. Who is worried about the plan?   3. What does the urban planner say?

2. Why is the person worried?   4. How does the person respond?

5 PAIR WORK **What are the two sides to the argument? What is your opinion about the proposal?**

> The urban planner wants to make the street more pedestrian-friendly.

> That seems like a good idea to me.

SMART TALK *What would you do?* **Student A:** Turn to page 91.
Student B: Turn to page 103.

READING

1 BEFORE YOU READ Look at the photo. What is happening?

INTERGENERATIONAL SCHOOLS GET HIGH MARKS

Ms. Beryl and Layla are great friends. It doesn't matter that Beryl is 87, and Layla is four. The pair have many interests in common, and they spend a lot of time together. They make drawings, play games, and laugh at each other's jokes.

The two attend an intergenerational preschool called, Mother Nurture. It is located in a retirement home, and it brings society's oldest and youngest members together in a cross-generational community.

"At Mother Nurture the kids have someone who can tell great stories, but who also has the time and patience to really listen to them," says director, Penny Livingston. "Many of the children do not have grandparents in the same city, and their friendships with their elderly 'classmates,' expose them to people at a different stage of life."

For the elderly, the experience is also rewarding. The children bring the joy and excitement of youth into their lives, and studies suggest that the time spent with preschoolers improves their overall well-being. Older participants report feeling less lonely, a serious problem among the elderly. Their

minds work better, and even their bodies seem to benefit from the contact with the children because they move more.

Mother Nurture is just one of many such programs that have appeared around the world. First begun in Japan, intergenerational programs are now in Europe, North America, Australia, and many other countries. The programs work and even the middle generation benefits. Many families do not have relatives nearby, and the opportunity for their children to spend time with a grandmotherly or grandfatherly figure pleases parents.

"When we do get together with family, Layla makes straight for her grandmother, climbs into her lap and asks for a story," says Layla's mother. "Having her at Mother Nurture has given her a good feeling about older people."

Many care providers agree, "We kind of get stuck with people who are the same age as us," says Maya, a caregiver who has worked at Mother Nurture for three years, "When I see how careful the children are around their older friends, I know they are developing empathy for people who are different," she says. "And that is good news for the rest of us since we will all be old one day."

2 Read the article. What is special about Mother Nurture?

3 Read the article again. Choose the correct answers to complete the sentences.

1. Old people and children meet in class at **a school / a retirement home**.

2. Old people are **healthier / more tired** after spending time with children.

3. Many children become **closer / less close** to their own grandparents after attending the school.

4. You can find intergenerational programs in **one country / many countries**.

5. Caregivers say that the programs teach children to have **empathy / patience**.

WRITING Turn to page 111.

SPEAKING *Where do you belong?*

1 **PAIR WORK** These people do not like where they live. What do you recommend for each one?

> I graduated from college last spring, and I am living with my parents in a small town. I miss my friends and the energy of the city.

> My wife and I just had a baby. We love our downtown apartment, but it's just getting too crowded.

> My husband and I need a change. Our children have gone to college and we are bored and lonely in our big house in the suburbs.

Sofía

Ryo

Linda

> If Sofía got a job and moved to the city, she'd be happier.

> Ryo and his wife might be more comfortable if they traded homes with Linda and her husband

2 What about you? Read the survey. Number the lifestyle choices in order of importance.

I would be happier if . . .	
I had more friends in my neighborhood.	
I could go to restaurants, sports events, and concerts more easily.	
there were lively art and music scenes nearby.	
there were more public parks and bicycle paths in my area.	
the neighborhood were quieter and had less traffic.	
I lived in the countryside without any neighbors.	
I lived in a home with bigger rooms and more outside space.	
there were more public transportation.	

3 **PAIR WORK** Discuss your choices in the survey. Then recommend a neighborhood or area to your partner. Explain what they could and couldn't do there.

4 **CLASS ACTIVITY** Share your responses. Which lifestyle choices are the most popular in your class? Which are least popular?

GO ONLINE
for grammar, vocabulary, and speaking practice

5 **OVER TO YOU** Find a real proposal for changing your neighborhood, town, or city. Do you think the proposal is a good idea? Tell a classmate.

NOW I CAN

SPEAKING	GRAMMAR	LISTENING	READING
☐ describe good / bad points about a neighborhood.	☐ use the second conditional.	☐ understand a town hall meeting.	☐ understand intergenerational schools.

55

09 | What would you have done?

SPEAKING
Regrets and solutions
GRAMMAR
Should have / would have
LISTENING
Realizing mistakes
READING
How to avoid regrets

VOCABULARY

 1 Look at the picture. How would you describe the way the people feel? Write the correct letter. Then listen and check your answers.

> **a.** irritated **b.** amused **c.** sympathetic **d.** embarrassed **e.** confused **f.** inconsiderate

WARMUP
Who do you go to for advice?

2 Complete the chart with the words in the box. Then add more words from the picture.

> hurt   helpful   uncomfortable   grateful
> rude   relieved   thoughtful   shocked

Positive	Negative

VOCABULARY TIP

Group new words by theme.

Positive: amused, sympathetic, ...

Negative: irritated, embarrassed, ...

3 **PAIR WORK** Tell your partner about a time when you made a mistake.

A I forgot my coworker's name.

B Oh no, I've done that, too. I was embarrassed!

CONVERSATION

HE CALLED ME TODD!

🎥 1:32

 1 Complete the conversation. Then watch and check your answers. Practice the conversation with a partner.

> **a.** grateful   **b.** Actually   **c.** Todd   **d.** embarrassed

Hannah So are you settling in okay? How has your first day been?

Scott It was all good except for one thing. Mr. Shafer called me by the wrong name. My name is Scott, and I don't know if you noticed, but he introduced me as **1**＿＿＿＿＿＿＿＿.

Hannah Oh no! That's awkward!

Scott And I was kind of **2**＿＿＿＿＿＿＿＿, so I never corrected him.

Hannah Oh, Scott! Why didn't you say something?

Scott I couldn't. I thought it would be rude.

Hannah Rude? No. He probably would have been **3**＿＿＿＿＿＿＿＿ that you told him.

Scott So, what would you have said?

Hannah Right away, I would have said, "**4**＿＿＿＿＿＿＿＿, I'm Scott."

Scott Yeah, I guess you're right. I should have done that!

 2 PAIR WORK Practice the conversation again. Use the ideas below. Add your own ideas.

1	2	3	4
Simon	uncomfortable	relieved	Sorry
Sam	confused	glad	In fact
＿＿＿＿＿	＿＿＿＿＿	＿＿＿＿＿	＿＿＿＿＿

 3 OVER TO YOU Work in pairs. Make a video of your conversation. Talk about an uncomfortable experience.

Student A Describe the experience.

Student B Show support and ask for details.

LANGUAGE PRACTICE

> ### Should have and would have
> Grammar Reference page 122
>
> What **should** I **have** done?
> You **should have said** something.
> I **should have done** that!
> You **shouldn't have done** that.
>
> What **would** you **have** said?
> I **would have said**, "I'm Scott."
> He **would have been** grateful.
> I **wouldn't have ignored** the mistake.

1 Complete the sentences. Use *should have* or *shouldn't have* and the verb in parentheses.

1. I'm so sorry! I _____ *should have sent* _____ (send) a thank-you note sooner.

2. I _____ (give) my boss my number. Now she calls me on Sundays!

3. We _____ (call) Kim on her birthday. I hope she isn't hurt.

4. Tom _____ (post) those embarrassing photos of me.

5. I apologize. We _____ (tell) you the meeting was canceled.

2 Put the words in the correct order to make sentences and complete the conversations.

1. **A** Jaylin borrowed Lionel's car and didn't put gas in the tank.

   B filled / I / have / would / tank / the _____ .

2. **A** Astrid was upset because her roommate left her clothes on the floor.

   B not / She / upset / have / about that / gotten / should _____ .

3. **A** Jon broke up with Hannah over text.

   B Really? I / have / would / done / in person / it _____ .

4. **A** Did you see how mad Lucas got when I left the door unlocked?

   B Yes. yelled / have / not / should / at / He / you _____ .

5. **A** My coworker quit yesterday because she wants to go back to school.

   B that / made / I / have / not / would / choice _____ .

3 **PAIR WORK** Tell a partner what you would have done in the situations in activity 2.

> I would have filled the tank, too!

> Yes, I would too. I would also have gotten upset about the clothes being on the floor.

PRONUNCIATION *Reduction of* wouldn't have / shouldn't have

1 Listen. Notice the reduced sounds of *wouldn't have* and *shouldn't have*.

Unreduced	Reduced
1. You shouldn't have done that.	You /ʃʊdntəv/ done that.
2. I wouldn't have ignored him.	I /wʊdntəv/ ignored him.
3. He shouldn't have bought a gift.	He /ʃʊdntəv/ bought a gift.
4. I wouldn't have told her that.	I /wʊdntəv/ told her that.

2 Listen again and repeat. Try to say the reduced forms.

LISTENING

1 **BEFORE YOU LISTEN** Complete the sentences with the correct words.

| confidence | honest | overcome | interfere |

1. Good workers _____ problems in order to do well.
2. You should always be _____ with your friends.
3. Don't _____ with your customers' personal lives.
4. Successful people have a lot of _____.

2 Listen to the people talking. Choose the correct answer.

1. What mistake did Kim and Mina make?
   a. They got involved in the personal lives of customers.
   b. They mixed up menus and gave them to the wrong customers.
2. What mistake did Eric make?
   a. He forgot to meet his friend at the library.
   b. He lied to his friend about his plans.
3. What mistake did Andrew make?
   a. He didn't go to a convention.
   b. He lied to his boss when he missed work.

3 Listen again. Choose (✓) *True* or *False*.

	True	False
1. Kim and Mina work in a print shop.	☐	☐
2. Jeff is Kim and Mina's boss.	☐	☐
3. Cathy and Eric play basketball together.	☐	☐
4. Eric had a party.	☐	☐
5. Andrew works in sales.	☐	☐
6. Andrew is nervous about flying.	☐	☐

4 **LISTENING PLUS** Listen to the people talking about their mistakes. Choose the correct answers.

1. Jeff is **irritated by / grateful to** his employees. Kim **apologizes / quits her job.**
2. Cathy is **embarrassed by / confused about** Eric's lie. By the end, Eric feels **relieved / hurt** by Cathy's response.
3. Andrew was **happy with / shocked by** his class. Now, he feels **comfortable / stressed** about traveling.

5 **GROUP WORK** What does each person learn from his / her mistake? What will they do or not do in the future?

> Kim learned she shouldn't have interfered. Next time, she won't ...

SMART TALK *Ask Ariana?* | **Student A:** Turn to page 92.
Student B: Turn to page 104.

READING

1 **BEFORE YOU READ** Look at the title. What do you think the author's purpose is?

    a. to inform the reader   **b.** to make the reader laugh   **c.** to advise the reader

How to Avoid Regret   *By Susan Quinn*

Regret is a **painful** emotion that hits us after a poor decision. We can't go back and change the past, but perhaps we can learn from mistakes and behave differently in the future. We asked readers to tell us about their regrets and the decisions that they don't regret. Let's see if you can find the lesson in these stories.

Elsa Q: My friend's mother was in the hospital for a month. I was really busy at work at the time and did not visit her. This was a woman who fed me, drove me to the beach, and came to my high school **graduation**. These thoughts all came to my mind after she was back home. My friend said it wasn't a big deal, but I should have visited her.

Jon F: One Saturday morning, my son and I had bought two beautiful cartons of fresh berries at the market when we saw a **homeless** person. We decided to give him a box of strawberries. To this day, I will never forget the look of pleasure on his face as he bit into one.

Sophie E: One of my roommates lost her job and needed a computer to do job applications. She didn't ask to borrow my laptop directly, but I knew she was going to the library every day to use the computers there. I should have let her borrow mine.

Charlie B: I was riding my bicycle across a parking lot entrance, when a driver, who was talking on her phone, nearly hit me. She tried to make an **excuse**, but I said, "If you had hit me, you would have felt really bad!" And then she **burst into tears** and apologized. I didn't want to make her cry, but I hope that I prevented her from hurting or killing someone.

Did you get the lesson? If you saw that the people who acted out of kindness to others had fewer regrets than the people who didn't, then you are right. People generally experience a happy memory after acts of generosity, and **unpleasant** memories when they are **thoughtless**. Who would ever regret being kind?

2 Read the article. Does the person feel regret or not? Find evidence in the article to support your answer.

	regret	no regret	evidence
1. Elsa			
2. Jon			
3. Sophie			
4. Charlie			

3 Read the article again. What is the main message of the article? Choose (✓) the correct answer.

☐ You will be very sad if people don't help you when you need something.

☐ If you have a good excuse for being thoughtless, you won't have regrets.

☐ If you are sympathetic and caring towards others, you will have fewer regrets in life.

4 **GROUP WORK** What are some decisions that you don't regret? Share your stories.

> I don't regret having my friend's daughter to stay with us when she started working in Bogotá.

WRITING Turn to page 112.

SPEAKING · *The should've / would've game*

1 Look at the directions and questions on the board game. Think about possible answers.

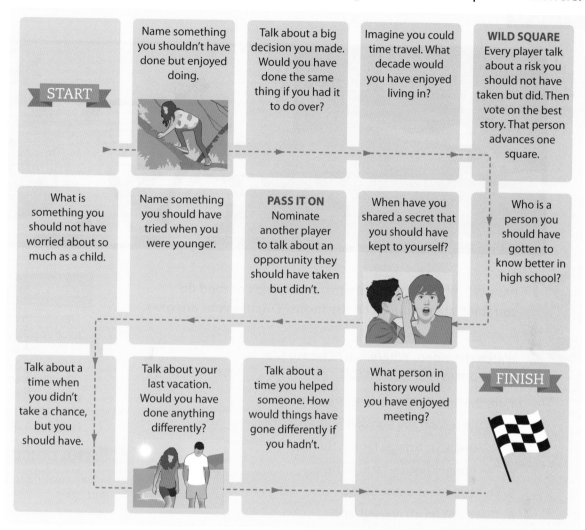

START

Name something you shouldn't have done but enjoyed doing.

Talk about a big decision you made. Would you have done the same thing if you had it to do over?

Imagine you could time travel. What decade would you have enjoyed living in?

WILD SQUARE Every player talk about a risk you should not have taken but did. Then vote on the best story. That person advances one square.

What is something you should not have worried about so much as a child.

Name something you should have tried when you were younger.

PASS IT ON Nominate another player to talk about an opportunity they should have taken but didn't.

When have you shared a secret that you should have kept to yourself?

Who is a person you should have gotten to know better in high school?

Talk about a time when you didn't take a chance, but you should have.

Talk about your last vacation. Would you have done anything differently?

Talk about a time you helped someone. How would things have gone differently if you hadn't.

What person in history would you have enjoyed meeting?

FINISH

Flip a Coin!   Heads ⚪ = move 1 space   Tails ⚫ = move 2 spaces

2 **GROUP WORK** Play the game. Answer the directions or questions on the squares that you land on. The first person to reach FINISH is the winner.

> Name something you shouldn't have done, but enjoyed doing.

> That's easy. When I was a kid, I often read comic books instead of doing my homework. I shouldn't have done it, but it was fun!

3 **OVER TO YOU** Find a picture of someone being saved from a difficult situation. What should the person have done? What would you have done? Tell a classmate.

GO ONLINE for grammar, vocabulary, and speaking practice

SPEAKING	GRAMMAR	LISTENING	READING
☐ talk about regrets and solutions to problems.	☐ use *should have / would have*.	☐ understand people realizing their mistakes.	☐ understand an article about regrets.

VIDEO

1:32

Growing Cities

1 **PAIR WORK** Look at the photos. What kinds of food do you think are produced on the farms? Discuss your answers.

2 Watch the video. Where is it? Choose (✓) New York (*NY*) or Detroit (*D*)?

	NY	D
1. It's the first city Dan and Andrew visit.	☐	☐
2. It's the second city Dan and Andrew visit.	☐	☐
3. The Brooklyn Grange farm is there.	☐	☐
4. The Brother Nature farm is there.	☐	☐
5. There's a lot of unused land.	☐	☐
6. There isn't much unused land.	☐	☐

Culture Tip

The most widely produced crop in the USA is corn, with over 90 million acres grown. Most of the corn is used to feed farm animals.

USEFUL LANGUAGE

urban: relating to towns and cities

3 Watch the video again. Write True (*T*), False (*F*), or Not Given (*NG*).

1. Most of the food grown in Nebraska now isn't for people to eat. ____
2. Dan and Andrew are going to visit ten urban farms around the USA. ____
3. The number of people living in Detroit has gone up over the years. ____
4. In Detroit, it's difficult to buy good-quality, fresh food. ____
5. In Nebraska, there isn't much unused land. ____
6. Brooklyn Grange farm is on a one-acre rooftop. ____
7. Brooklyn Grange farm sells vegetables to restaurants in New York. ____

4 **PAIR WORK** Discuss the questions.

1. If you visited the Brother Nature Farm and Brooklyn Grange, what questions would you ask Greg and Anastasia?
2. If you started an urban garden,...

   ...where would it be?   ...what would you grow there?   ...what would you do with the produce?

> I would ask Greg, "Can you explain why you started the farm?"

> I'd ask Anastasia, "Can you tell me how many eggs the chickens lay?"

READING

 1 PAIR WORK Look at the title of the article and the photos. What do you think the article is about?

THE GREENER, THE BETTER

The number of people living in cities has been rising year after year. Today, over half of the world's population lives in urban areas. As a result, many cities have had valuable green spaces removed to accommodate the extra people.

This is worrying, as these green areas would have been useful in many ways. They would have improved people's health, by making air quality better and providing outdoor space for relaxation and exercise. They would have helped fight climate change, by reducing carbon levels and urban temperatures. And they would have provided homes for wildlife, such as birds and bees.

Thankfully, many cities are now doing the opposite and developing projects to create more green spaces.

One example is the *High Line* in New York. This 2.3-kilometer-long public park was built on a disused rail line. When the train service stopped, the plan was to have the elevated railway demolished. Fortunately, however, the public fought to save the structure. The park has over 500 types of plants and trees, as well as many artworks and design features. Each year, around five million visitors appreciate this wonderful green space.

Another project is the *Parc Rives de Seine* in Paris. What used to be busy multi-lane expressways on either side of the river have been closed to vehicle traffic. In their place are now seven kilometers of pathways and parkland for pedestrians and cyclists to enjoy. There are also outdoor sports facilities, art installations, and performance spaces. Another feature is the *Floating Garden*, which is five islands, each growing different plants and flowers.

By 2050, it is expected that over two-thirds of the world's population will live in urban areas. If more creative projects like these were introduced, it would ensure more clean, green urban spaces for future generations.

🔊 **2** Read the article. Answer the questions.

1. Why have many cities lost green spaces?
2. Why are green spaces good for people's health?
3. In what ways are the *High Line* and the *Parc Rives de Seine* similar?
4. In what ways are the *High Line* and the *Parc Rives de Seine* different?
5. In the future, is the number of people living in cities going to increase or decrease?

3 GROUP WORK Discuss the questions.

1. Would you prefer to visit the *High Line* or the *Parc Rives de Seine*? Explain why.
2. What could be done to make your hometown greener?
3. Why do you think more and more people are choosing to live in urban areas?

10 | Anything's possible.

SPEAKING
Speaking on the past
GRAMMAR
Modals + *have*
LISTENING
Conspiracy theorists
READING
Hoaxes

WARMUP
Have you ever seen something you couldn't explain?

VOCABULARY

 1 Look at the website. How would you describe these things? Write the correct letter. Then listen and check your answers.

a. fact-checker   c. hoax   e. prediction

b. mystery   d. conspiracy theory   f. doctored photo

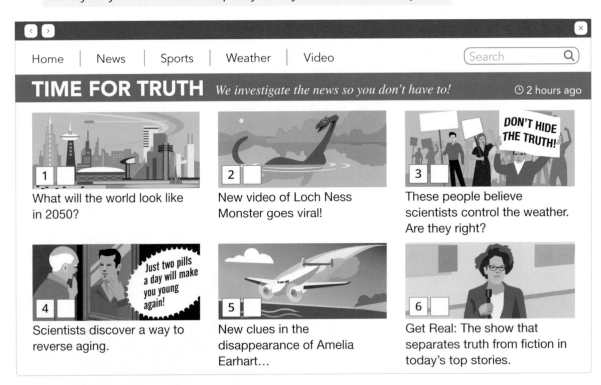

| Home | News | Sports | Weather | Video | Search 🔍 |

TIME FOR TRUTH *We investigate the news so you don't have to!*   ⏱ 2 hours ago

1 What will the world look like in 2050?

2 New video of Loch Ness Monster goes viral!

3 These people believe scientists control the weather. Are they right?

DON'T HIDE THE TRUTH!

4 Scientists discover a way to reverse aging.

Just two pills a day will make you young again!

5 New clues in the disappearance of Amelia Earhart…

6 Get Real: The show that separates truth from fiction in today's top stories.

2 Complete the chart with the words in the box. Then add more words from the website.

rumor   urban legend   myth   proof   explanation   scam   evidence   fact

True	Might be fake	Fake

3 **PAIR WORK** Talk about the items on the *Time for Truth* website. What do you think about them?

What do you think about the Loch Ness Monster story?

It's clearly a doctored photo and a fake video!

64

CONVERSATION

IT'S NOT REAL!

1:32

1 Complete the conversation. Then watch and check your answers. Practice the conversation with a partner.

a. camping   b. seem   c. Check out   d. a fake photo

Adam   Hey, Amy! **1** _____ this photo. Do you see that bear chasing the photographer? It's about 20 feet tall!

Amy   A 20-foot-tall bear, Adam? That's **2** _____ !

Adam   I don't know. Bears can come in different sizes. Maybe this one is a giant bear just like sometimes there are giant people.

Amy   There's Patrick. Look Patrick. What do you think of that bear?

Patrick   I've seen that photo before. Someone must have used software to make a regular bear **3** _____ bigger. It's not real, Adam.

Adam   How do you know for sure?

Patrick   If it were real, there would be more evidence.

Amy   I don't know why anyone would post something like that!

Patrick   They may have wanted it to go viral. It's a way to get attention.

Adam   Well, either way, I'm not **4** _____ in those woods!

2 PAIR WORK Practice the conversation again. Use the ideas below. Add your own ideas.

1	2	3	4
Have a look at	a doctored photo	look	hiking
Come see	a hoax	appear	walking
_____	_____	_____	_____

3 OVER TO YOU Work in pairs. Make a video of your conversation. Talk about strange photos or videos.

Student A   Describe an unusual real or fake photo or video.

Student B   Ask for more information to find out if it was real or fake.

CONVERSATION TIP

BEING POLITE
When you want to disagree politely, you can give a neutral response.

That's a fake photo!

I don't know.

65

LANGUAGE PRACTICE

May, might, could, and must have   Grammar Reference page 123

Uncertain

Someone **may have wanted** it to go viral.

It **could have been** a hoax.

It **might have been** a fake photo.

The witness **may not have told** the truth.

It **might not have been** real.

Certain

Teenagers **couldn't have done** it.

Someone **must have used** software to doctor the photo.

I **must not have seen** it clearly in the dark.

1 Choose the correct phrases to complete the sentence.

1. That noise (must have) / couldn't have been the wind. No one else is here.

2. Joe saw the ghost, too. So it **may have / couldn't have** been a dream.

3. He **might not have / must not have** checked the facts carefully. Amelia Earhart was definitely born in 1897.

4. I didn't see the object clearly, but it **must have / could have** been a drone!

5. Suwei **must have / might have** quit the band, but I'm not sure.

2 Rewrite the conversation using *may, might, could,* or *must have.*
More than one answer is sometimes possible.

A Did you hear that someone saw a monster in Mirror Lake?

B Yes. I'm sure it was a hoax. _____ .

A I don't know. It looked real in the picture.

B It was probably a doctored photo. _____ .

A Why would they do that?

B Maybe they wanted to sell it to a news site. _____ .

3 PAIR WORK Write conversations for these mysteries.

| strange lights in the sky | a dark shape under the ocean | a large crash in a desert |

A I saw strange lights in the sky.

B They must have been drones.

A I don't know. They were moving too fast.

PRONUNCIATION *Reduction of* have *after modals*

1 Listen. Notice the reduced sound of the helping verb *have* after modals.

Unreduced

1. It /kʊdəv/ been an alien.

2. They /maɪtəv/ used boats.

3. It /məstəv/ been a scam.

4. They /meɪyve/ been here.

Reduced

It /kʊdə/ been an alien.

They /maɪtə/ used boats.

It /məstə/ been a scam.

They /meɪyə/ been here.

2 Listen again and repeat. Try to say the reduced forms.

LISTENING

1 **BEFORE YOU LISTEN** Match the headlines to the pictures.

1

2

3

A **NEWS**

New book exposes the **hidden forces** controlling the Internet.

B ☒

Restaurant manager fired for making **false claims** about food safety practices.

C

Scientists report the **negative consequences** of taking too many vitamins.

 2 Listen to the podcast. Choose the correct definition for a conspiracy theorist according to the listening.

1. They don't need an explanation for things that happen, they sometimes fact check, they like to work alone. They are the only ones who know the truth.

2. They need an explanation for things that happen, they always fact check so they can be sure about their story, and they share their beliefs with other people.

3. They need an explanation for things that happen, they choose only the details that fit their story, and they form connections with people who have the same beliefs.

 3 Listen again. Choose (✓) *True* or *False*.

	True	False
1. Dr. Howard and Dr. Chin talk about human behavior.	☐	☐
2. A conspiracy theorist will change their story if presented with scientific evidence.	☐	☐
3. The show's guests believe that doctors hide the negative effects of medicine.	☐	☐
4. According to the show's guests, educated people can be conspiracy theorists.	☐	☐
5. The World Health Organization (WHO) recommends that people eat less meat.	☐	☐
6. Conspiracy theories are always fake.	☐	☐

4 **LISTENING PLUS** Listen to the rest of the podcast. Answer the questions.

1. How does Bill do his research?

2. What information does Bill share?

3. What does Dr. Howard suggest Bill reads?

4. How does Bill respond to this suggestion?

5. How do you think Dr. Howard and Dr. Chin would describe Bill?

5 **GROUP WORK** What do you know about conspiracy theorists? Discuss.

I think conspiracy theorists can be helpful, but not always.

I'm worried that they might share the wrong information and confuse people.

SMART TALK *Mysterious places* | **Student A:** Turn to page 93. **Student B:** Turn to page 105.

READING

1 BEFORE YOU READ Why are there so many hoaxes these days?

HOAX BUSTERS *Fact or Fiction? Send us your questions, and we'll do the research.*

What is a gorilla crow?

I saw a video of a crow that had a bird's face and the body of a gorilla, or at least it looked like a gorilla. I usually dismiss these videos as hoaxes, but this was on a news show on TV at a restaurant, and the sound was turned off, so I thought it might have been real.
– Mercedes V.

FICTION: There is no bird called a gorilla crow, but the video you saw is **authentic**, and the crow is real. The bird was probably spreading its wings to warm up or clean its feathers. The feet were not **visible** because of the camera angle. That position also made the crows wings look like gorilla arms, but the photo was not doctored.

Can you charge your phone with an onion?

I watched a video where a man charged his phone with an onion. He cut holes in the onion. Then he connected the power cord, and the phone started charging! I was not convinced, but the video looked so real, so now I'm not sure. Can vegetables produce electricity?– Tyler

FICTION: Vegetables have many benefits, but producing electricity is not one of them. Don't be **fooled** by the onion video. The man **pretended** to use science, but it's a hoax.

Building melts car?

I've heard that the light reflecting off a glass window can be hot enough to melt a car. Is that a fact or an urban legend?– Emma

FACT: Surprisingly, it has happened. In London, a skyscraper made the news when it melted parts of a car parked across the street. The building's unique shape had turned its glass windows into a mirror, raising temperatures on the street to 60 degrees Celsius. The builders apologized to the owner of the car and are working to fix the problem.

2 Read the article. Write *H* (hoax) or *F* (fact) for the sentences.

1. There is a bird called a gorilla crow that can stand on its wings. ____

2. You can charge a phone with an onion. ____

3. A glass building can make enough heat to melt parts of a car. ____

3 PAIR WORK Read the article again. Answer the questions and discuss with a partner.

1. Which situation shows something that happens in nature?

2. Why did the writer believe that vegetables might produce power?

3. Which situation was an accident and not a hoax?

4. What did the builders do when they found out about the car?

4 GROUP WORK Discuss these questions.

- Which of these stories surprised or didn't surprise you?

- Why do you think people make hoaxes?

WRITING Turn to page 112.

SPEAKING *It could have been a doctored photo!*

1 Write the correct news headline underneath the photos.

- Neighbors Report Seeing Strange Creatures in Local Forest
- Melting Snow Reveals a Mysterious Object
- Guest Sees Ghost in Hotel Hallway
- Hikers Photograph Hairy Monster

1. _____

3. _____

2. _____

4. _____

2 GROUP WORK Discuss the photos and the headlines. What might people have seen? Think of real and unreal explanations.

> Picture number 1 could be a photo of a real ghost. It looks so real!

> Yeah, but don't you think someone could have doctored it?

3 PAIR WORK Tell your partner about an interesting mystery or theory you know. What do you think of it? Why?

> My friend says he believes there is a monster in Loch Ness, but I don't because...

4 OVER TO YOU Find a photo of a hoax to share with the class. Tell the story.

GO ONLINE
for grammar, vocabulary, and speaking practice

NOW I CAN

SPEAKING	GRAMMAR	LISTENING	READING
☐ speculate about mysteries and the past.	☐ use modals + *have*	☐ understand conspiracy theorists.	☐ understand stories about hoaxes.

11

What would have happened?

SPEAKING
Describing inventions
GRAMMAR
Third conditional
LISTENING
New inventions
READING
How inventors work

VOCABULARY

WARMUP
What are three inventions you could not live without?

 1 Look at the pictures. What things do you see? Write the correct letter. Then listen and check your answers.

a. tool   b. gadget   c. appliance   d. instrument   e. utensil   f. gear

---

THE SMARTEST INVENTIONS *at the Best Prices!*

1
Soundarino
The two-in-one electronic Soundarino is a must-have for the musician in your life.

2
Spoonsticks
One end is a spoon, the other chopsticks!

3
Leo the laundry bot
No more wrinkled clothes

4
Bugaway hat and gloves
Go fishing, hiking, camping and more, with our wearable mosquito proof products.

5
Tri-Cam
It can fly, swim, and trek! Open up a whole new world of photography

6
See in the dark wrench
Now you can work when the electricity goes out.

---

2 Complete the chart with the words in the box. Then add more words from the website.

| device | create | develop | contraption |
| adapt | improve | innovate | breakthrough |

Things inventors do	Inventions

VOCABULARY TIP

Learn different forms of a new word.

Adapt (verb)

Adaptation (noun)

Adaptable (adjective)

3 **PAIR WORK** What are your favorite inventions? Tell your partner.

> I think the Bugaway hat and gloves is great for being out in the mountains. I wish I had one.

CONVERSATION

IT DOESN'T WORK!

1:32

1 Complete the conversation. Then watch and check your answers. Practice the conversation with a partner.

    a. Hey   **b.** confusing   **c.** play music   **d.** device

Alan   Hello? Hello?

Diana   Hey, what's wrong?

Alan   It's this stupid **1** _____. My daughter got it for me, and I can't get it to work!

Diana   That was nice of her. Maybe I can help. What do you want it to do?

Alan   It's supposed to do things for me like **2** _____. If I had known it was so hard to use, I would have returned it.

Diana   Oh, I have one of these. It's a digital assistant. You talk to it, and it talks back.

Alan   Yeah, but it doesn't answer. These things are so **3** _____.

Diana   Here, let me help. Hmm. Maybe you just have to say the right thing. Hello, Erica.

Device   Hi, how can I help you today?

Alan   **4** _____, you did it! Erica! Erica, can you hear me?

Device   Yes, I can hear you.

2 PAIR WORK Practice the conversation again. Use the ideas below. Add your own ideas.

1	2	3	4
gadget	turn on the lights	annoying	Woo hoo!
contraption	check the weather	unclear	Hooray!
_____	_____	_____	_____

3 OVER TO YOU Work in pairs. Make a video of your conversation. Talk about a problem with a new device.

Student A   Complain about a new device.

Student B   Ask questions about the device. Give advice.

LANGUAGE PRACTICE

> **Third conditional**   Grammar Reference page 124
>
> If I **had known** it was so hard to use, I **would have returned** it.
>
> If you **had invented** it, what **would** you **have done**?
>
>   If I **had invented** it, I **could have made** a lot of money.
>
> I probably **wouldn't have done** anything if I'd **had** the idea.
>
> If I **had told** her the price, she **would have been** angry.
>
> I **wouldn't have brought** this tool if I'**d known** you had one.
>
> If she **hadn't been** an inventor, she **might have been** an artist.
>
> NOTE: I had → I'd

1   Read the sentences. Write *T* (true) or *F* (false).

1. If I had known about the smart refrigerator, I would have tried to get one.

  _F_ **a.** I knew about the refrigerator.

____ **b.** I didn't try to get one.

2. If he had read the report, he wouldn't have bought Leo the laundry bot.

____ **a.** He read the report.

____ **b.** He didn't buy Leo the laundry bot.

3. You wouldn't have lost the gadget if you'd known how to track it.

____ **a.** You lost the gadget.

____ **b.** You knew how to track it.

4. If we hadn't encouraged her, she might not have sold her invention.

____ **a.** We encouraged her.

____ **b.** She sold her invention.

2   **PAIR WORK** Ask and answer the questions.

1. How would you have felt if you had invented the airplane?

2. How would your childhood have been different if the television hadn't been invented?

3. What would you have done if you had lived 100 years ago?

4. How would your life be different if no one had discovered electricity?

PRONUNCIATION   *Changing syllable stress*

1   Listen. Notice how the syllable stress changes in different parts of speech in some words and notice how it doesn't change in others.

	Verb	Adjective	Noun
Change	1. a**dap**t	a**dap**table	adap**ta**tion
	2. **inn**ovate	**inn**ovative	inno**va**tion
No change	3. pre**dict**	pre**dict**able	pre**dic**tion
	4. cre**ate**	cre**a**tive	cre**a**tion

2   Listen again and repeat. Try to stress the correct syllable.

LISTENING

1 **BEFORE YOU LISTEN** Complete the sentences with the correct words.

futuristic   practical   portable   ingenious

1. When something is _____ , you can carry it from place to place.

2. A technology that might be possible such as a flying car is _____ .

3. People like _____ innovations because they make life easier.

4. When we really admire the creativity of an invention, we say it's _____ .

2 Listen to people describing new inventions. Write the correct invention.

Mini-Medi Lab   Chef Pot   Friendix

1. The _____ is good for people who need a home assistant.

2. The _____ gives step-by-step instructions.

3. The _____ doesn't need electricity to work.

3 Listen again. Answer the questions.

1. a. What does the Chef Pot do for cooks?
   b. What kind of person would buy this pot?

2. a. What are three tasks the Friendix can do?
   b. What can't it do yet?

3. a. Who invented the Mini-Medi Lab and why?
   b. What does it do?

4 **LISTENING PLUS** Listen to two callers. Select (✓) the statements that match Pete's advice.

☐ **1.** You need to find a community.

☐ **2.** In a maker space, you can get help from other inventors.

☐ **3.** You should keep your ideas secret no matter what.

☐ **4.** All you need to make your invention is a good idea.

☐ **5.** To invent something, it's important to have skills and tools.

5 **PAIR WORK** If you had been a judge, which invention would you have awarded first, second, and third place?

READING

1 **BEFORE YOU READ** Look at the photo. What do you think "a Eureka moment" is?

HOW TO CREATE A EUREKA MOMENT

For years, people have tried to find the secret to invention. An idea always seems obvious once someone else has it, but it wasn't before. The rolling suitcase, sunglasses, windshield wipers, or an app that puts cat ears on selfies. Where would we be without these inventions?

It turns out that many inventors simply change, improve, or **repurpose** existing products. For example, Henry Ford created an **efficient** way to produce cars, but previous inventors had already put engines onto carriages. Steve Jobs did not invent the mouse. An engineer had introduced the device to the computing world 25 years before. Jobs simply improved it and introduced it to the general public.

Another feature of invention is **collaboration**. When people have different areas of **expertise**, they can share ideas and solutions to problems. Universities may partner with industry and government to create research opportunities and labs. These centers attract different experts who then combine their knowledge and skills. Sometimes these "hubs" **specialize** in a particular type of invention. One may focus on medical breakthroughs such as **artificial** arms and legs that people can control with

their minds. Another might develop green solutions such as **solar panels** that can be placed on roads to collect energy from the sun.

Such hubs can now be found all over the world from the Haidian District in Beijing, to Station F in Paris. Others can be found online in the form of open source projects, which invite anyone to work on a solution or design without pay. In these virtual communities the pleasure of solving problems and developing something new drives invention.

So if you want to be an inventor, these are the steps you can take. Then through **exploration**, conversation, and experimentation, you might just find yourself saying, "Eureka" because you created the next big thing.

2 Read the article. Select (✓) the best summary.

- [ ] A successful inventor thinks differently from other people and finds new markets for his / her invention.
- [ ] A successful inventor makes current inventions work in new or better ways, shares ideas and solutions with other experts, and enjoys solving problems.
- [ ] A successful inventor makes existing products better, works alone for long periods of time, and enjoys solving problems.

3 Read the article again. Answer the questions.

1. How did Henry Ford improve the automobile?
2. What did Steve Jobs change about the computer mouse?
3. Who do invention hubs attract?
4. What are some examples of specialized hubs?
5. Why do people work for open source projects without pay?

4 **GROUP WORK** What sort of invention hub interests you? What sorts of inventions would you like to work on?

> I would like to work for a robotics hub.
> I like engineering and programing!

WRITING Turn to page 113.

SPEAKING *What couldn't you live without?*

1 **PAIR WORK** Circle the inventions you've used in the past three days. Discuss how you used them.

- the smartphone
- the computer
- the microwave
- the car

- the ATM
- sunglasses
- the refrigerator
- (your idea)

2 **GROUP WORK** Take turns asking how your life would have been different without the inventions in activity 1.

- this morning
- yesterday
- last weekend
- last summer

- the last time you took a vacation
- the last time you went shopping
- the last time you...

> If no one had invented sunglasses, how would your life have been different last summer?

> If sunglasses hadn't been invented, I wouldn't have enjoyed the beach, and I couldn't have read books.

3 **CLASS ACTIVITY** Discuss and decide which three inventions in activity 1 are the most important. How would your lives be different without them?

4 **OVER TO YOU** Find out the history of an important invention. Who invented it? When? Share your research in small groups.

GO ONLINE
for grammar, vocabulary, and speaking practice

NOW I CAN

SPEAKING	GRAMMAR	LISTENING	READING
☐ discuss life with and without inventions.	☐ use the third conditional.	☐ understand descriptions of new inventions.	☐ understand how inventors work

12 | Did you hear the news?

SPEAKING
Describing news
GRAMMAR
Reported speech
LISTENING
News stories
READING
The nature of news

VOCABULARY

1 Look at the picture. What do you see? Write the correct letter. Then listen and check your answers.

a. article   c. citizen journalist   e. weather report   g. headline

b. news site   d. camera operator   f. breaking news   h. reporter

2 Complete the chart with the words in the box. Then add more words from the picture.

editor   update   column   politics   blogger   broadcast   journalist   business

News people	Things they produce	Subjects they cover

 GROUP WORK How do you get your news? Which is the most popular way?

• website   • social media   • newspaper   • television   • radio

CONVERSATION

THAT'S GOT TO BE A MISTAKE!

1:32

 1 Complete the conversation. Then watch and check your answers. Practice the conversation with a partner.

> **a.** reporter **b.** warn **c.** article

Scott These trees are really beautiful.

Carlos Did you see that **1** _____ about how trees communicate with each other?

Scott But that's crazy! Trees don't even know how to think, so how can they talk?

Carlos No, it's true. I didn't say talk. I said they communicate.

Scott And what does that mean?

Carlos Well, I'll explain. It depends on how you define communicate. This **2** _____ said that trees share information through their roots.

Scott But what information does a tree share?

Carlos Well, it said that they **3** _____ each other about harmful insects. The first tree produces chemicals the insects hate, and the other trees learn to produce the same chemicals and share their recipe with other trees in the forest.

Scott I don't know about that. Where's this story from?

Carlos A nature magazine. The writer interviewed a forest manager who wrote a book about it. Apparently, trees are smarter than we realize.

 2 **PAIR WORK** Practice the conversation again. Use the ideas below. Add your own ideas.

1	2	3
story	blogger	tell
column	journalist	inform
_____	_____	_____

 3 **OVER TO YOU** Work in pairs. Make a video of your conversation. Talk about a news story.

Student A Share a news story.

Student B Ask about the story and where your partner heard about it.

CONVERSATION TIP

GIVING MORE DETAILS
Give more details to explain the information in a news story.

> Where's this story from?

> A nature magazine. The reporter said ...

LANGUAGE PRACTICE

Reported speech	Grammar Reference page 125
Direct	**Reported**
"Trees **share** information through their roots."	It said (that) trees **share** information through their roots.*
"What does that mean?"	He asked what that **meant**.
"It **isn't** fair."	He said (that) it **wasn't** fair.
"It **came** from a nature magazine."	He said (that) it **had come** from a nature magazine.
"I **spoke** to a journalist at my house."	She said she **had spoken** to a journalist at her house.
"I**'ll** turn off the TV."	She said (that) she **would** turn off the TV.
"He **can** afford it."	She told him (that) he **could** afford it.
"**Was** the robber **caught**?"	He asked if the robber **had been caught**.
"Where **did** you see the article?"	She asked me where I **had seen** the article.

* *When you want it to be clear that something is still true or a general truth, you don't need to make tense changes.*

1 Rewrite the sentences as reported speech. Change tenses and pronouns.

1. "I'm not interested in sports." She said _(that) she wasn't interested in sports_ .

2. "I won't tell anyone your secret." She told us _____ .

3. "I work in a zoo." He said _____ .

4. "I haven't read the article yet." I told her _____ .

2 Complete the reported questions with *who, what, where,* or *if*. Then write the direct questions.

1. I asked her _____ she got her news. "_____ ?"

2. He asked her _____ kinds of shows she watched. "_____ ?"

3. She asked him _____ he had ever gone snowboarding. "_____ ?"

4. They asked her _____ she would like to meet. "_____ ?"

3 CLASS ACTIVITY Ask and answer questions from activity 2 with a partner. Then tell the class what you learned about your partner.

> My partner told me he got his news from social media.

PRONUNCIATION *Contrastive stress*

1 Listen. Notice the stress on words that are compared.

1. He told me he hadn't <u>seen</u> the accident; he <u>heard</u> it.

2. She said she <u>doesn't</u> read the newspaper, but she <u>does</u> listen to the radio.

3. He said he'll do his homework <u>before</u> the movie, not <u>after</u>.

4. She told us the tickets cost <u>$35 each</u>, not <u>$45 each</u>.

2 Listen again and repeat. Try to stress the compared words.

LISTENING

1 BEFORE YOU LISTEN Complete the headlines with words from the box.

rescue	protesters	oppose	contagious

1. Angry _____ fill the streets to _____ the city's plan to close a local hospital.

2. Centers for Disease Control creates a hotline for _____ diseases.

3. Local fishermen _____ family after their boat turns over in a storm.

2 Listen to three news stories. Number the headlines in the order you hear their stories.

_____ a. Protestors resist plan to destroy historic library building.

_____ b. Rescuers working to bring fallen kindergartener out of a six-meter hole in the ground.

_____ c. Hospitals see increase in patients with mysterious flu-like symptoms.

3 Listen again. Choose the correct answers to complete the sentences.

1. Serena Novak was walking with her **parents / grandmother** when she fell into a hole.

2. Rescuers were able to send **a flashlight / food** to the trapped child.

3. A mysterious illness is causing **dizziness / breathing problems**.

4. People with symptoms should call **their doctor / the Centers for Disease Control**.

5. Central Library is a **100- / 300-** year-old building.

6. The library's board of directors want to **tear down / save** the building.

4 LISTENING PLUS Listen to the updates. Choose (✓) *True* or *False*.

	True	False
1. Serena Novak was rescued.	☐	☐
2. The mysterious disease is contagious.	☐	☐
3. The library board of directors tried to have a secret meeting	☐	☐
4. The Central Library building was torn down.	☐	☐

5 GROUP WORK Do you think the Serena Novak story is important breaking news? What news stories do you think are the most important?

> The library story is important. Historic buildings should be saved.

> Maybe you're right, but I think it's important to know about illnesses!

SMART TALK *What did she say?* | Student A: Turn to page 95. | Student B: Turn to page 107.

READING

1 **BEFORE YOU READ** What was the last piece of news you heard? Was it good or bad news?

Why Is the News
SO DARK?

Storms, disease, crime, and other disasters attract readers' and viewers' attentions. These are the things we think of when we think of news. A study by Canadian researchers found that people are more likely to choose to read negative news when looking through a news site. This **attraction** even has a name: **negativity bias.**

In fact, people's attraction to bad news has a useful purpose. It is a **survival** strategy that goes back to the days of lions and tigers. When someone said they had seen a lion, others needed to pay attention. Today people still pay attention when the news reports danger but for another reason. If there is a news story about a big fire, people want to know the details. This information **satisfies** a **curiosity** about the drama of the situation. It might also be useful if they experience a fire in their own home as well, of course.

However, when people see a lot of bad news there can also be negative **consequences.** We live in a world with a 24-hour news cycle, so photographs and headlines that cause anger or fear tend to follow us through the day and stick in our memory. They become topics of conversation and may even lead us to false beliefs and make bad decisions. For example, top stories about plane crashes may cause people to fear flying. Although few people fear driving, it is far more dangerous than flying.

The psychologist, Stephen Pinker, is worried that this negative world view can make people believe the world is getting worse. They may lose **trust** in leaders or fear people who are different. Pinker points out that there have been many positive changes recently: for example, more people are living longer and healthier lives **overall.** However, as those types of changes generally happen slowly over time, they don't make headlines.

Pinker says that it is important to be aware of negativity bias and to realize that headlines may not have messages of peace, but that doesn't mean all countries are at war.

2 Read the book excerpt. Choose (✓) *True* or *False*.

	True	False
1. Negativity bias is the idea that people often choose to read bad news over good news.	☐	☐
2. Bad news is good for helping people prepare for threats.	☐	☐
3. Experts agree that negativity bias is always good.	☐	☐
4. News can influence people to make bad decisions.	☐	☐
5. Stephen Pinker believes that the world is getting worse.	☐	☐

3 Read the excerpt again. Answer the questions.

1. How does the 24-hour news cycle affect people?
2. What is a negative effect of a news story about a plane crash?
3. What does Dr. Pinker want people to remember about the news?

4 **GROUP WORK** Share your opinions. What is the best way to get the news? Why?

> I like to read the news online because I can compare different news sites and leave comments.

 WRITING Turn to page 113.

SPEAKING *Breaking news*

1 **GROUP WORK** In groups of three, discuss what you think happened in these news stories.

2 **GROUP WORK** In your groups, choose a story and take roles so that one is a reporter and two are people in the story. Then role play an interview.

ROLES	REPORTERS
Story 1 Big storm: Prepare to tell the story of how a tree fell on your house.	Ask the couple who, what, when, where questions about the storm.
Story 2 Movie star rescue. Prepare to tell the story of how a movie star rescued a swimmer.	Ask who, what, when, where, questions about the rescue.
Story 3 Citizen Hero. Prepare to tell the story of how you put out a fire in the neighborhood.	Ask who, what, when, where how questions about the fire.

3 **CLASS ACTIVITY** Reporters take turns reporting the news stories to the class.

> The actor said he had been sailing when he heard a cry for help.

GO ONLINE
for grammar, vocabulary, and speaking practice

4 **OVER TO YOU** Find information about a recent news event. Report the news event to a classmate.

NOW I CAN

SPEAKING	GRAMMAR	LISTENING	READING
☐ talk about news events.	☐ use reported speech.	☐ understand news stories.	☐ understand the nature of news.

VIDEO

The Climate Heroes

1 **PAIR WORK** Look at the photos. What climate problems can you think of? What do you think a 'Climate hero' might do? Discuss your answers with your partner.

Culture Tip

Climate is the long-term pattern of weather in a particular area. The Earth has three main climate zones—tropical, temperate, and polar.

2 Watch the video. Choose the correct words to complete the summary.

In the video, six children from ¹ **Colorado / California** take part in a competition. They think of a local climate problem, a connection to another place in the ² **country / world** with a similar problem and then find a solution. The group's idea is to put cameras which use energy from the ³ **sun / wind** into forests. The cameras are connected to the Internet, so ⁴ **students / the public** at home can help detect forest fires. The group ⁵ **wins / doesn't win** the competition.

3 Watch the video again. Match the person—narrator (*N*), male student (*M*), female student (*F*)—to what he / she said.

Who said ...?

1. the summer had been terrible because of the fires. _____
2. their global connection was Spain because they had the same climate. _____
3. the group had been selected to go to the international competition. _____
4. anyone could be a Forest Guard. _____
5. he / she thought there was a fire in the picture. _____
6. the young people had shown they were ready to build a better future. _____

4 **PAIR WORK** Discuss the questions. Listen carefully to what your partner says.

1. What are the biggest climate problems in your country?
2. Which other places in the world have similar problems?
3. Can you think of any solutions to these problems?

5 **PAIR WORK** Find a new partner. Tell him / her what your previous partner said.

> Rosa said she thought the biggest climate problem in her country was flooding.

READING

1 PAIR WORK Look at the article. What is the purpose of the article?

THE WORLD'S WEIRDEST INVENTOR

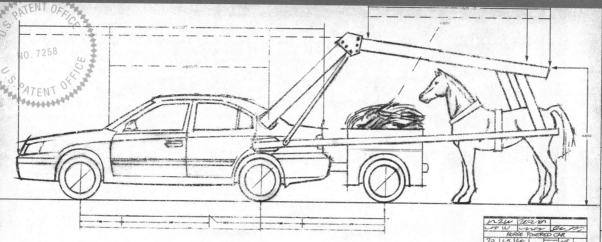

A patent is a government document that says you are the inventor of a gadget, device, or idea. The world's most famous inventor, Thomas Edison, owned over 1,000 patents. Many of these patents were for breakthroughs that changed our world, like the lightbulb. The world's most prolific inventor is an Australian man named Kia Silverbrook. He has over 3,000 patents–more than anyone in the world. His patents are related to printers, including a tiny printer in a phone.

If Edison was the most famous inventor and Silverbrook is the most prolific, then the strangest inventor must have been a British man named Arthur Pedrick. Pedrick patented over 160 peculiar contraptions in the 1960s and 1970s. He invented a bicycle you could ride underwater, a golf ball you could steer in the air, and a machine that shoots snowballs from Antarctica to the Australian desert.

Some of Pedrick's creations sound like jokes, or even hoaxes, like a horsepowered automobile, a car you drive from the back seat, or a flying saucer. In his patent applications, he often talks about his cat, Ginger. However, Pedrick couldn't have been crazy. He had worked in the UK's patent office. He gave clear explanations for everything, and his ideas were based on real scientific theories and phenomena.

Although Pedrick's inventions could have worked, none of them were ever actually made into products. If he had tried to produce them, it would have cost billions of dollars. Also, if he'd tried to sell them, he might not have found many buyers. Finally, Pedrick's wife got tired of all of the equipment in the house and told her husband to stop inventing. Just imagine: If she hadn't stopped him, what else would Pedrick have invented?

 2 Read the article. Answer the questions.

1. What inventors does the article mention? How are they different?
2. What are three of Arthur Pedrick's inventions? What do they do?
3. Does the writer of the article think Pedrick is crazy? Why or why not?

 3 GROUP WORK Would you use any of Pedrick's inventions? Why or why not?

> I'd like to try the car you can drive from the back seat. It sounds a little scary, but also exciting!

SMART TALK   UNIT 1 *Personal profiles*

Student A

1 **PAIR WORK** Ask and answer questions to complete the information.

  A How long has Jen been living in Chicago?

  B She's been living there since 2017.

JEN GOMEZ

Lives in: Chicago (since ___2017___)

Hobby: Playing violin (for five years)

Right now: I've been organizing my _____ since I woke up!

MINSEO PAK

Lives in: _____ (since I graduated)

Hobby: Taking Spanish classes (since last year)

Job: Teaching English (for _____)

ERIC SANTOS

Job: Baking cakes (for _____)

Hobby: Making videos (since my baby son was born!)

Lives in: _____ (since 2018)

MIA GOLD

Job: Making apps (for two years)

Hobby: Playing tennis (since _____)

Right now: I've been working on an app all night.

CHARLES BISSET

Lives in: Montreal (since I was born)

Hobby: _____ (since I retired)

Right now: I've been visiting my grandchildren all week.

SAM LIU

Lives in: Shanghai (since last year)

Hobby: Taking _____ (since I moved to China)

Right now: I've been practicing kicks!

---

2 Ask about your partner. Complete the sentences.

  1. My partner's been studying English since _____ .

  2. My partner's been living in his / her home for _____ .

  3. My partner's been _____ since he / she can remember.

  4. My partner's been _____ for more than five years.

  5. My partner's been _____ all day!

  6. My partner hasn't been _____ recently.

UNIT 2 *What do you want to watch?*

Student A

1 PAIR WORK Ask and answer questions to complete the show and movie guides. Use indirect questions. Decide which show you both want to watch.

A Do you know what *Like Me* is about?

B It's about a man who runs a dating service.

A Huh, well, that might be good.

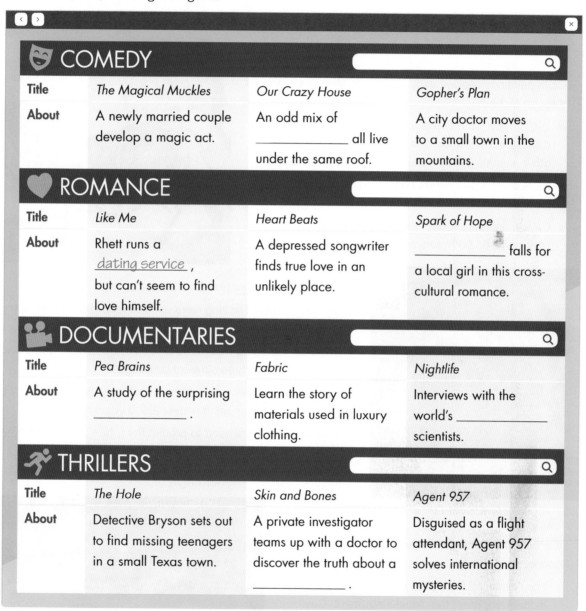

🎭 COMEDY

Title	The Magical Muckles	Our Crazy House	Gopher's Plan
About	A newly married couple develop a magic act.	An odd mix of _____ all live under the same roof.	A city doctor moves to a small town in the mountains.

♥ ROMANCE

Title	Like Me	Heart Beats	Spark of Hope
About	Rhett runs a _dating service_ , but can't seem to find love himself.	A depressed songwriter finds true love in an unlikely place.	_____ falls for a local girl in this cross-cultural romance.

🎥 DOCUMENTARIES

Title	Pea Brains	Fabric	Nightlife
About	A study of the surprising _____ .	Learn the story of materials used in luxury clothing.	Interviews with the world's _____ scientists.

🏃 THRILLERS

Title	The Hole	Skin and Bones	Agent 957
About	Detective Bryson sets out to find missing teenagers in a small Texas town.	A private investigator teams up with a doctor to discover the truth about a _____ .	Disguised as a flight attendant, Agent 957 solves international mysteries.

2 Ask about your partner. Complete the sentences.

1. My partner and I never watch _____ .

2. We both hate _____ .

3. We both watch _____ .

4. My partner likes _____ , but I don't.

UNIT 3 *Art and archeology*

Student A

1 **PAIR WORK** Ask and answer questions to complete the information.

    A When were the Lascaux cave paintings discovered?

    B They were discovered in 1940.

Art and archeology

CAVE ART

Cave paintings allowed early humans to share experiences through pictures.

- __In 1940__ the Lascaux cave paintings were discovered in France. The pictures of the horses and other animals were painted nearly 20,000 years ago.

- Cave paintings of hands and a kind of deer in Sulawesi, Indonesia were painted about _____ years ago.

- Cave paintings in Spain were made by the ancestors of humans 65,000 years ago.

ANCIENT WRITING

Many early forms of writing were used to record business, but they were also used as historical and legal documents.

- The Rosetta Stone was made around _____ years ago. It was written in three different languages.

- The Cyrus Cylinder was written on soft clay. It tells the story of a famous Persian ruler. It is over 2,500 years old.

- Oracle bones were used to predict the future in ancient China. They show an early writing system that is more than 3,000 years old.

THE FIRST MUSIC

It is believed that music helped people form social connections.

- The Australian Aboriginal instrument, the didgeridoo, is not the oldest instrument. Cave paintings of the instrument are only about _____ years old.

- Metal bells were first made in China around 2,600 years ago. They were used to find animals and in religious ceremonies.

- A flute made from the wing of a bird was found in Germany. It is about _____ years old.

UNIT 4 *She's the one who ...*

Student A

1 PAIR WORK Look at the applicants for a job at a middle school. Ask and answer the questions to complete the information.

A Who is Jeff Olson?

B He's the one who sponsors the nature club.

Jeff Olson

Double major in biology and education

Six years' experience teaching science.

Sponsor of the _____nature_____ club.

Cora Walters

Degree in _____ .

Three years teaching language arts.

Awarded best teacher in _____ .

Olga Michaels

Degree in math.

_____ years teaching experience.

Coach for the Math Olympiad competition.

Sponsor of the computer science club.

Farouk Khan

Ph.D in _____ management.

One-year teaching experience.

Certificate in educational leadership.

Volunteers at the public _____ .

Sooyun Park

Degree in music.

_____ years teaching experience.

Ten years graphic design experience.

2 Then choose the best candidate for each job. Give reasons for your choices.

A I think Farouk is someone who could be principal.

B Yes, but Olga has experience that will be useful for ...

Job descriptions for the next academic year	Offer the position to
A sixth-grade language arts teacher	
A seventh-grade science teacher	
Performing and visual arts program director	
Coordinator of the honors program for science, technology, engineering, and math (STEM)	
Principal for the school	

UNIT 5 *Apps for active people*

Student A

1 **PAIR WORK** Ask and answer questions to complete the information. Use *to* and *for* and the correct form of the verb.

A Can you use *Helpish* for scheduling meetings?

B Yes, you can. Can you use DRIVE-WAYS to schedule meetings?

	Helpish	DRIVE-WAYS	Braineroo
1. for / schedule meetings	yes	no	_____
2. to / organize travel plans	yes	_____	no
3. for / play games	_____	no	_____
4. to / give directions	yes	_____	no
5. to / learn vocabulary	_____	no	_____
6. to / avoid traffic	yes	_____	no
7. for / find restaurants	_____	yes	_____
8. for / do math problems	yes	_____	yes
9. to / make group chats	_____	no	_____
10. to / post photos	yes	_____	yes

2 Ask and answer questions to complete the sentences about the apps you use.

1. My partner uses _____ to play games.

2. My partner uses _____ to get directions.

3. We both use _____ for sending messages.

4. We both use _____ for searching the Internet.

5. My partner uses _____ for checking the weather.

6. My partner uses _____ to listen to music.

UNIT 6 *By the time she was 18, …*

Student A

1 PAIR WORK Ask and answer questions to complete the information.

A What had Ricky learned to do by the time he was 18?

B He'd learned to climb mountains.

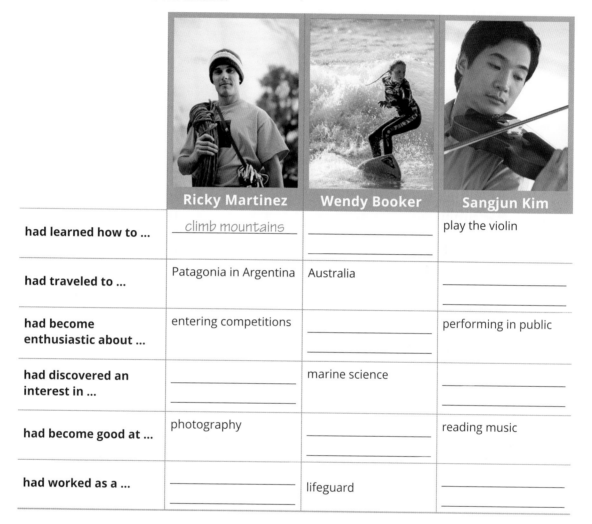

	Ricky Martinez	Wendy Booker	Sangjun Kim
had learned how to …	*climb mountains*		play the violin
had traveled to …	Patagonia in Argentina	Australia	
had become enthusiastic about …	entering competitions		performing in public
had discovered an interest in …		marine science	
had become good at …	photography		reading music
had worked as a …		lifeguard	

2 Ask about your partner. Complete the sentences.

1. By the age of five, my partner and I had both learned how to _____ .
2. My partner had traveled to _____ by the age of _____ .
3. By the age of _____ , my partner had become enthusiastic about _____ .
4. By the age of 10, my partner and I had both discovered an interest in _____ .
5. My partner had become good at _____ by the age of _____ .

UNIT 7 *Before and after*

Student A

1 **PAIR WORK** How did the people change their homes? Look at the *before* picture. Ask your partner what the people had done. Then look at the *after* picture and answer your partner's questions. Use the words in the boxes.

A Did Macarena get her stove repaired?

B Yes, she did.

1. repaired	2. painted	3. cleaned	4. replaced

Macarena's home

1. cut	2. trimmed	3. repaired	4. planted

Jun and Harin's yard

UNIT 8 *What would you do?*

Student A

1 PAIR WORK Ask your partner questions and write their responses. Then answer your partner's questions.

A If you had to live on a desert island, who would you bring with you?

B I would bring my family.

	My response	My partner's response
1. If you had to live on a desert island, who would you bring with you?		
2. If you could be an expert on any subject, what would you choose?		
3. If you could have any job in the world, what would it be?		
4. If your house was on fire, what one thing would you save?		
5. If you could have a superpower, what would it be?		
6. If you could live anywhere in the world, where would you live?		
7. If you could have many friends or a lot of money, which would you choose?		
8. If you could time travel, would you go to the past or the future?		
9. If you could help solve any problem in the world, what problem would you like to solve?		
10. If you could have a special talent such as painting or singing, what talent would you choose?		

2 Compare your answers. Are you mostly similar or mostly different?

1. What are two or three things you have in common?

2. What are two or three ways you are different?

> Both of us would choose to be singers. We'd like to travel the world and give concerts.

91

UNIT 9 *Ask Ariana?*

Student A

1 **PAIR WORK** Ask and answer questions to complete the information.

A What would John never have known if he had stayed in his small town?

B He never would have known that he can't recognize faces.

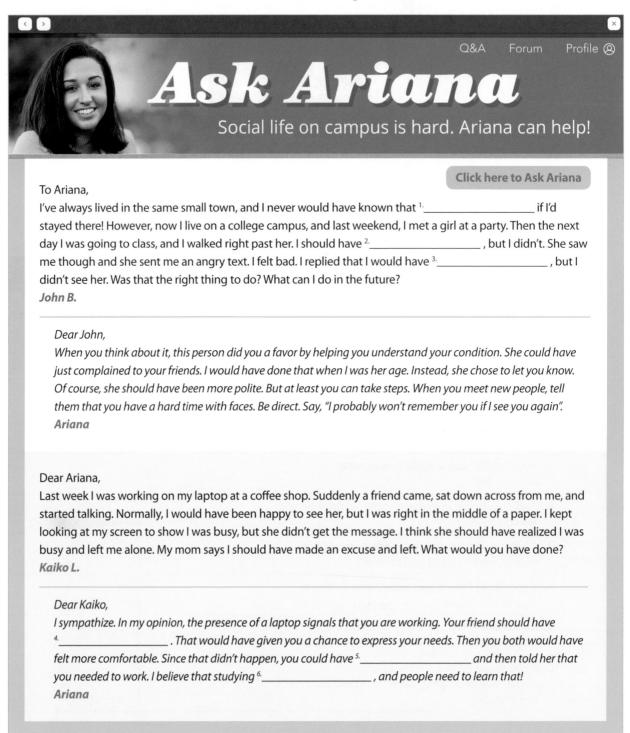

Q&A   Forum   Profile ⊗

Ask Ariana

Social life on campus is hard. Ariana can help!

Click here to Ask Ariana

To Ariana,

I've always lived in the same small town, and I never would have known that ¹·_____ if I'd stayed there! However, now I live on a college campus, and last weekend, I met a girl at a party. Then the next day I was going to class, and I walked right past her. I should have ²·_____ , but I didn't. She saw me though and she sent me an angry text. I felt bad. I replied that I would have ³·_____ , but I didn't see her. Was that the right thing to do? What can I do in the future?

John B.

Dear John,

When you think about it, this person did you a favor by helping you understand your condition. She could have just complained to your friends. I would have done that when I was her age. Instead, she chose to let you know. Of course, she should have been more polite. But at least you can take steps. When you meet new people, tell them that you have a hard time with faces. Be direct. Say, "I probably won't remember you if I see you again".

Ariana

Dear Ariana,

Last week I was working on my laptop at a coffee shop. Suddenly a friend came, sat down across from me, and started talking. Normally, I would have been happy to see her, but I was right in the middle of a paper. I kept looking at my screen to show I was busy, but she didn't get the message. I think she should have realized I was busy and left me alone. My mom says I should have made an excuse and left. What would you have done?

Kaiko L.

Dear Kaiko,

I sympathize. In my opinion, the presence of a laptop signals that you are working. Your friend should have ⁴·_____ . That would have given you a chance to express your needs. Then you both would have felt more comfortable. Since that didn't happen, you could have ⁵·_____ and then told her that you needed to work. I believe that studying ⁶·_____ , and people need to learn that!

Ariana

2 Discuss the answers to these questions with your partner.

- Do you agree with Ariana's advice? Why or why not?
- What else could the people have done in these situations?

UNIT 10 *Mysterious places*

Student A

 1 PAIR WORK Read about Yonaguni. Then answer your partner's questions.

YONAGUNI

- Yonaguni is an island on the southwestern tip of the Japanese archipelago. It is famous because of rock formations under the water.

- The Yonaguni Monument, as it is called, was first discovered by divers in 1986. They saw rock structures, and they thought they might have been made by humans.

- Ocean scientists and archeologists began to explore the site. There are three different theories about how the monument could have been formed.

- The first theory believes that the Yonaguni Monument could have been built about 10,000 years ago when there was a land bridge connecting Yonaguni to Taiwan. They think it could have been the site of the mythical city of Mu.

- A second theory says that the site could have been built 5,000 years ago and then sank into the ocean. They say that some drawings on rocks are similar to the Kaida script which was used on these islands at that time.

- A third theory is that the site wasn't built by humans. Researchers think the formations must have been created by frequent earthquakes in the area that could have broken rocks and made a structure that looks like an ancient city.

- The area has become a popular spot for divers.

2 Ask your partner about Giant's Causeway. Complete the sentences.

Where is Giant's Causeway?

1. Giant's Causeway is a mysterious set of rocks on the coast of _____ .
2. The rocks form columns that fit together like tiles and cover _____ miles of coastline.
3. The name comes from a story about an ancient _____ named Finn McCool.
4. Finn built the causeway to cross the water to _____ .
5. He wanted to _____ with his enemy Benandonner, but then he must have changed his mind because he came back quickly.
6. When Benandooner followed him back across the water, McCool's wife pretended her husband was her _____ .
7. McCool's plan must have worked because Benandonner left and _____ the causeway.
8. In reality, the causeway must have been made by _____ 50–60 million years ago.
9. Melted rock must have _____ and _____ into the hexagonal shapes.

UNIT 11 *Who invented it?*

Student A

1 **PAIR WORK** Ask and answer questions to complete the information.

A Who invented the umbrella?

B The people of the Cao Wei Dynasty in China.

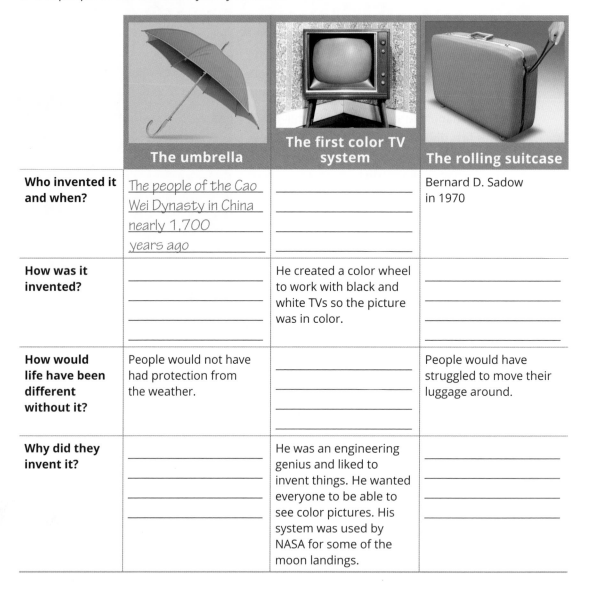

	The umbrella	The first color TV system	The rolling suitcase
Who invented it and when?	The people of the Cao Wei Dynasty in China nearly 1,700 years ago		Bernard D. Sadow in 1970
How was it invented?		He created a color wheel to work with black and white TVs so the picture was in color.	
How would life have been different without it?	People would not have had protection from the weather.		People would have struggled to move their luggage around.
Why did they invent it?		He was an engineering genius and liked to invent things. He wanted everyone to be able to see color pictures. His system was used by NASA for some of the moon landings.	

2 Ask and answer the questions. How would live have been different if the following had not been invented?

emojis   the camera   headphones   (your own idea) _____

How would life have been different if emojis had not been invented?

Humans would not have had a way to show their feelings when they text.

UNIT 12 *What did she say?*

Student A

1 PAIR WORK Ask and answer questions to complete the article. Use reported speech.

A What is Dr. Amano working on?

B She's working on a new supercomputer.

Scientist Gives Back to **Local School**

The award-winning scientist, Kim Amano is setting up an after-school program at her childhood elementary school. The Las Palmas Weekly spoke to her about her work and her charity.

Q: Thank you for your time, Dr. Amano. I've heard that you are working on a new
1 _supercomputer_ . Can you tell us about it?

A: Well, one thing is that we want to be better at predicting the 2. _____ .
Right now, it's very hard to do that because there is so much data

Q: And a big computer will help you with that?

A: Yes, if we can use information from weather balloons and satellites better, we can warn people about heat or a 3. _____ .

Q: Do you need a lot of math?

A: Of course, but also 4. _____ , and people do not always realize that.

Q: Is that why you set up the computer science program? To help students
5. _____ between computers and their own lives?

A: Absolutely. Computers are our best 6. _____ for solving problems.
When we combine them with things like weather, or medicine, or …

Q: … or 7. _____ ?

A: Yes, that too. We can meet the challenges of the 21st century. For example, they'll do research on
8. _____ right here in Las Palmas.

Q: That sounds like a great experience. I'm sure the community is grateful for your contributions both in science and in 9. _____ .

A: Thank you!

2 Ask and answer the questions with a partner.

1. What did Dr. Amano say about using super computers?

2. What did Dr. Amano say about computer science and creativity?

3. What do you think about Dr. Amano's ideas?

95

Student B

1 PAIR WORK **Ask and answer questions to complete the information.**

A How long has Jen been living in Chicago?

B She's been living there since 2017.

JEN GOMEZ

Lives in: Chicago (since 2017)

Hobby: Playing _____violin_____ (for five years)

Right now: I've been organizing my music since I woke up!

MINSEO PAK

Lives in: Seoul (since I graduated)

Hobby: Taking Spanish classes (since _____)

Job: Teaching English (for five months)

ERIC SANTOS

Job: Baking cakes (for ten years)

Hobby: Making videos (since _____!)

Lives in: London (since 2018)

MIA GOLD

Job: Making apps (for _____)

Hobby: Playing tennis (since I was five)

Right now: I've been working on an app _____ .

CHARLES BISSET

Lives in: _____ (since I was born)

Hobby: Doing volunteer work (since I retired)

Right now: I've been visiting _____ all week.

SAM LIU

Lives in: Shanghai (since _____)

Hobby: Taking kung fu classes (since I moved to China)

Right now: I've been practicing _____ !

2 **Ask about your partner. Complete the sentences.**

1. My partner's been studying English since _____ .

2. My partner's been living in his / her home for _____ .

3. My partner's been _____ since he / she can remember.

4. My partner's been _____ for more than five years.

5. My partner's been _____ all day!

6. My partner hasn't been _____ recently.

UNIT 2 *What do you want to watch?*

Student B

1 PAIR WORK Ask and answer questions to complete the show and movie guides. Use indirect questions. Decide which show you both want to watch.

A Do you know what *Like Me* is about?

B It's about a person who runs a dating service.

A Huh, well, that might be good.

	COMEDY		
Title	*The Magnificent Muckles*	*Our Crazy House*	*Gopher's Plan*
About	A newly married couple develop a _____magic_____ act.	An odd mix of college students all live under the same roof.	A _____ moves to a small town in the mountains.

	ROMANCE		
Title	*Like Me*	*Heart Beats*	*Spark of Hope*
About	Rhett runs a dating service, but he can't seem to find love himself.	A _____ finds true love in an unlikely place.	A tour guide falls for a local girl in this cross-cultural romance.

	DOCUMENTARIES		
Title	*Pea Brains*	*Fabric*	*Nightlife*
About	A study of the surprising intelligence of birds.	Learn the story of materials used in _____ .	Interviews with the world's top space scientists.

	THRILLERS		
Title	*The Hole*	*Skin and Bones*	*Agent 957*
About	Detective Bryson sets out to find _____ in a small Texas town.	A private investigator teams up with a doctor to discover the truth about a mysterious illness.	Disguised as a _____ , Agent 957 solves international mysteries.

2 Ask about your partner. Complete the sentences.

1. My partner and I never watch _____ .

2. We both hate _____ .

3. We both watch _____ .

4. My partner likes _____ shows, but I don't.

UNIT 3 *Art and archeology*

Student B

1 **PAIR WORK** Ask and answer questions to complete the information.

    A When were the Lascaux cave paintings discovered?

    B They were discovered in 1940.

Art and archeology

CAVE ART

Cave paintings allowed early humans to share experiences through pictures.

- In 1940 Lascaux cave paintings were discovered in France. The pictures of horses and other animals were painted nearly ___20,000___ years ago.

- Cave paintings of hands and a kind of deer in Sulawesi, Indonesia were painted about 40,000 years ago.

- Cave paintings in Spain were made by the ancestors of humans _____ years ago.

ANCIENT WRITING

Many early forms of writing were used to record business, but they were also used as historical and legal documents.

- The Rosetta Stone was made around 2,200 years ago. It was written in three different languages.

- The Cyrus Cylinder was written on soft clay. It tells the story of a famous Persian ruler. It is over _____ years old.

- Oracle bones were used to predict the future in ancient China. They show an early writing system that is more than _____ years old.

THE FIRST MUSIC

It is believed that music helped people form social connections.

- The Australian Aboriginal instrument, the didgeridoo, is not the oldest instrument. Cave paintings of the instrument are only about 1,500 years old.

- Metal bells were first made in China around _____ years ago. They were used to find animals and in religious ceremonies.

- A flute made from the wing of a bird was found in Germany. It is about 43,000 years old.

UNIT 4 *She's the one who ...*

Student B

1 PAIR WORK Look at the applicants for a job at a middle school. Ask and answer the
questions to complete the information.

B Who is Jeff Olson?

A He's the one who has a double major in biology and education.

Jeff Olson

Double major in
___biology___ and education.

Six years' experience
teaching science.

Sponsor of the nature club.

Cora Walters

Degree in education.

Three years teaching
_____ .

Awarded best teacher in
2020.

Olga Michaels

Degree in math.

20 years teaching experience.

Coach for the Math Olympiad
competition.

Sponsor of the _____
club.

Farouk Khan

Ph.D in business management.

One-year teaching
experience.

Certificate in _____
leadership.

Volunteers at the public
library.

Sooyun Park

Degree in _____ .

Twelve years teaching
experience.

Ten years _____
experience.

2 Choose the best candidate for each job. Give reasons for your choices.

A I think Farouk is someone who could be principal.

B Yes, but Olga has experience that will be useful for ...

Job descriptions for the next academic year	Offer the position to
A sixth-grade language arts teacher	
A seventh-grade science teacher	
Performing and visual arts program director	
Coordinator of the honors program for science, technology, engineering, and math (STEM)	
Principal for the school	

UNIT 5 *Apps for active people*

Student B

1 **PAIR WORK** Ask and answer questions to complete the information. Use *to* and *for* and the correct form of the verb.

A Can you use Helpish for scheduling meetings?

B Yes, you can. Can you use DRIVE-WAYS to schedule meetings?

	Helpish	DRIVE-WAYS	Braineroo
1. for / schedule meetings	yes	_____	yes
2. to / organize travel plans	_____	yes	_____
3. for / play games	no	_____	yes
4. to / give directions	_____	yes	_____
5. to / learn vocabulary	yes	_____	yes
6. to / avoid traffic	_____	yes	_____
7. for / find restaurants	yes	_____	no
8. for / do math problems	_____	no	_____
9. to / make group chats	yes	_____	yes
10. to / post photos	_____	yes	_____

2 Ask and answer questions to complete the sentences about the apps you use.

1. My partner uses _____ to play games.
2. My partner uses _____ to get directions.
3. We both use _____ for sending messages.
4. We both use _____ for searching the Internet.
5. My partner uses _____ for checking the weather.
6. My partner uses _____ to listen to music.

UNIT 6 *By the time she was 18, …*

Student B

1 PAIR WORK **Ask and answer questions to complete the information.**

A What had Ricky learned to do by the time he was 18?

B He'd learned to climb mountains.

	Ricky Martinez	Wendy Booker	Sangjun Kim
had learned how to …	climb mountains	ride a surfboard	_____ _____
had traveled to …	_____ _____	_____ _____	Fukuoka, Japan
had become enthusiastic about …	_____ _____	protecting the oceans	_____ _____
had discovered an interest in …	geology	_____ _____	traditional Korean music
had become good at …	_____ _____	swimming and diving	_____ _____
had worked as a …	server	_____ _____	music camp counselor

2 **Ask about your partner. Complete the sentences.**

1. By the age of five, my partner and I had both learned how to _____ .

2. My partner had traveled to _____ by the age of _____ .

3. By the age of _____ , my partner had become enthusiastic about _____ .

4. By the age of 10, my partner and I had both discovered an interest in _____ .

5. My partner had become good at _____ by the age of _____ .

UNIT 7 *Before and after*

Student B

1 **PAIR WORK** How did the people change their homes? Look at the *after* picture. Answer your partner's questions. Then look at the *before* picture and ask your partner what the people had done. Use the words in the boxes.

A Did Macarena get her stove repaired?

B Yes, she did.

| 1. repaired | 2. painted | 3. cleaned | 4. replaced |

Macarena's home

| 1. cut | 2. trimmed | 3. repaired | 4. planted |

Jun and Harin's yard

UNIT 8 *What would you do?*

Student B

◯1 PAIR WORK Ask your partner questions and write their responses.
Then answer your partner's questions.

A If you had to live on a desert island, who would you bring with you?

B I would bring my family.

	My response	My partner's response
1. If you had to live on a desert island, who would you bring with you?		
2. If you could be an expert on any subject, what would you choose?		
3. If you could have any job in the world, what would it be?		
4. If your house was on fire, what one thing would you save?		
5. If you could have a superpower, what would it be?		
6. If you could live anywhere in the world, where would you live?		
7. If you could have many friends or a lot of money, which would you choose?		
8. If you could time travel, would you go to the past or the future?		
9. If you could help solve any problem in the world, what problem would you like to solve?		
10. If you could have a special talent such as painting or singing, what talent would you choose?		

2 Compare your answers. Are you mostly similar or mostly different?

1. What are two or three things you have in common?

2. What are two or three ways you are different?

> Both of us would choose to be singers. We'd like to travel the world and give concerts.

UNIT 9 *Ask Ariana?*

Student B

1 **PAIR WORK** Ask and answer questions to complete the information.

A What would John never have known if he had stayed in his small town?

B He never would have known that he can't recognize faces.

‹ ›

Q&A   Forum   Profile 👤

Ask Ariana

Social life on campus is hard. Ariana can help!

Click here to Ask Ariana

Dear Ariana,

Last week I was working on my laptop at a coffee shop. Suddenly a friend came, sat down across from me, and started talking. Normally, I would have 1._____ , but I was right in the middle of a paper. I kept looking at my screen to show I was busy, but she didn't get the message. I think she should have realized 2._____ and left me alone. My mom says I should have 3._____ . What would you have done?

Kaiko L.

Dear Kaiko,

I sympathize. In my opinion the presence of a laptop signals that you are working. Your friend should have asked before sitting down. That would have given you a chance to express your needs. Then you both would have felt more comfortable. Since that didn't happen, you could have chatted briefly and then told her that you needed to work. I believe that studying should always come before friends, and people need to learn that!

Ariana

To Ariana,

I've always lived in the same small town, and I never would have known that I can't remember faces if I'd stayed there! However, now I live on a college campus, and last weekend, I met a girl at a party. Then the next day I was going to class, and I walked right past her. I should have remembered her face, but I didn't. She saw me though and she sent me an angry text. I felt bad. I replied that I would have said hello, but I didn't see her. Was that the right thing to do? What can I do in the future?

John B.

Dear John,

When you think about it, this person did you a favor by helping you understand your condition. She could have just 4._____ . I 5._____ when I was her age. Instead, she chose to let you know. Of course, she should have 6._____ . But at least, you can take steps. When you meet new people, tell them that you have a hard time with faces. Be direct. Say, "I probably won't remember you if I see you again".

Ariana

2 Discuss the answers to these questions with your partner.

- Do you agree with Ariana's advice? Why or why not?
- What else could the people have done in these situations?

UNIT 10 *Mysterious places*

Student B

1 **PAIR WORK** Read about the Giant's Causeway. Then answer your partner's questions.

GIANT'S CAUSEWAY

- Giant's Causeway is a mysterious set of rocks on the coast of Northern Ireland.

- The rocks form columns that fit together like tiles. Altogether, there are 400,000 columns of hexagonal stones along four miles of coastline.

- According to legend, the giant Finn McCool built the causeway in order to cross the water to Scotland to fight another giant named Benandonner.

- When McCool arrived, he must have been frightened by the size of his enemy because he came back quickly.

- When Benandonner followed him back, Finn McCool's wife pretended her husband was her baby son to frighten Benandonner into thinking the real Finn was much bigger.

- The plan must have worked because after Benandonner saw the baby McCool, he tore up the rocks of the causeway so McCool could not follow him back to Scotland.

- In fact, we now know that volcanoes must have made the causeway 50 to 60 million years ago

- Melted rock from the volcanoes cooled when it reached the sea, and it must have cracked into the hexagonal shapes we see today.

- The Giant's Causeway attracts 300,000 visitors each year.

2 Ask your partner about the mystery of Yonaguni. Complete the sentences.

Where is Yonaguni?

1. Yonaguni is an island on _____ of the Japanese archipelago.

2. It is famous because rock formations _____ may be a lost city.

3. In _____ , divers found rock structures.

4. Researchers have explored the site and come up with _____ different theories.

5. The first theory says that the Yonaguni Monument could have been built around 10,000 years ago when there was a _____ between the island and Taiwan.

6. They say it might have been _____ of Mu.

7. The second theory says it might have been built _____ years ago and that it sank into the ocean.

8. A third theory is that the site couldn't have been built by _____ .

9. _____ may have caused the rocks to break and made them look like an ancient city.

UNIT 11 *Who invented it?*

Student B

1 **PAIR WORK** Ask and answer questions to complete the information.

A Who invented the umbrella?

B The people of the Cao Wei Dynasty in China.

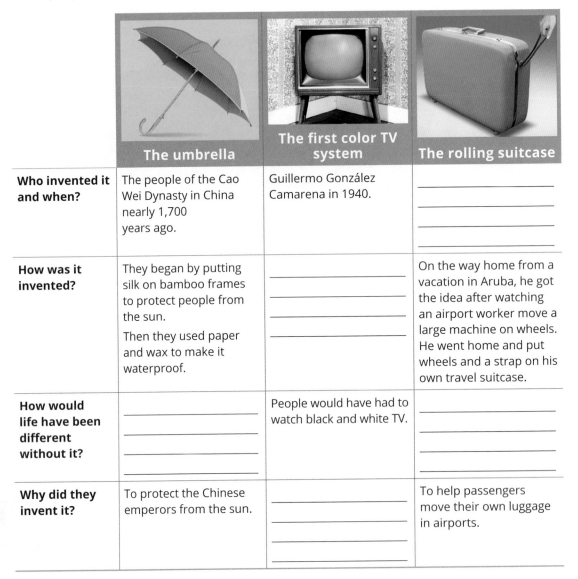

	The umbrella	The first color TV system	The rolling suitcase
Who invented it and when?	The people of the Cao Wei Dynasty in China nearly 1,700 years ago.	Guillermo González Camarena in 1940.	_____ _____ _____ _____
How was it invented?	They began by putting silk on bamboo frames to protect people from the sun. Then they used paper and wax to make it waterproof.	_____ _____ _____ _____	On the way home from a vacation in Aruba, he got the idea after watching an airport worker move a large machine on wheels. He went home and put wheels and a strap on his own travel suitcase.
How would life have been different without it?	_____ _____ _____ _____	People would have had to watch black and white TV.	_____ _____ _____
Why did they invent it?	To protect the Chinese emperors from the sun.	_____ _____ _____ _____	To help passengers move their own luggage in airports.

2 Ask and answer the questions. How would life have been different if the following had not been invented?

> emojis   the camera   headphones   (your own idea) _____

How would life have been different if emojis had not been invented?

Humans would not have had a way to show their feelings when they text.

UNIT 12 *What did she say?*

Student B

1 PAIR WORK Ask and answer questions to complete the interview. Use reported speech.

A What is Dr. Amano working on?

B She's working on a new supercomputer.

Scientist Gives Back to **Local School**

The award-winning scientist, Kim Amano, is setting up an after-school program at her childhood elementary school. The Las Palmas Weekly spoke to her about her work and her charity.

Q: Thank you for your time, Dr. Amano. I've heard that you are working on a new supercomputer. Can you tell us about it?

A: Well, one thing is that we want to be better at predicting the weather. Right now, it's very hard to do that because there is so much 1._____ .

Q: And a big computer will help you with that?

A: Yes, if we can use information from weather 2._____ and 3._____ better, we can warn people about heat or a big storm.

Q: Do you need a lot of 4._____ ?

A: Of course, but also creativity, and people do not always realize that.

Q: Is that why you set up the 5._____ program? To help students make connections between computers and their own lives?

A: Absolutely. Computers are our best tool for solving problems. When we combine them with things like weather, or 6._____ , or ...

Q: ... or rocket science?

A: Yes, that too. We can meet the challenges of 7._____ . For example, they'll do research on traffic patterns right here in Las Palmas.

Q: That sounds like a 8._____ . I'm sure the community is 9._____ for your contributions both in science and in education.

A: Thank you!

2 Ask and answer the questions with a partner.

1. What did Dr. Amano say about using supercomputers?
2. What did Dr. Amano say about computer science and creativity?
3. What do you think about Dr. Amano's ideas?

WRITING

UNIT 1

1 Look at the news site ad and read the email answering it. Then write an email about yourself to answer the ad. Remember to answer the following questions:

- What is your special talent?
- How long have you been performing?
- Why should you be on Stars on Stage?

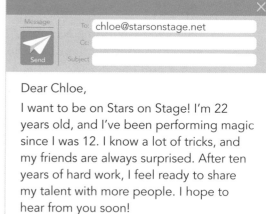

Dear Chloe,

I want to be on Stars on Stage! I'm 22 years old, and I've been performing magic since I was 12. I know a lot of tricks, and my friends are always surprised. After ten years of hard work, I feel ready to share my talent with more people. I hope to hear from you soon!

Sincerely,

Mulrooney the Great

2 **PAIR WORK** Compare your emails. Who should Chloe choose to be on the show?

UNIT 2

1 Read this post from a social media star. Then write a message to Kylie about a problem that you think should be her next big project.

2 **PAIR WORK** Compare your message with a partner. Then as a class vote on which problem should become Kylie's next project.

108

UNIT 3

1 Read this poster about Chapultepec Park. Then write an informational poster or brochure about a large park or public space that you know. Try to answer the following questions in your poster:

- Where is the park / space located?
- When was it built?

- What trees or gardens been planted there?
- What other attractions are there?

VISIT CHAPULTEPEC

El Bosque de Chapultepec is located in the center of Mexico City. This world-famous park is visited by 15 million people every year and is one of the oldest and largest urban parks in the world.

Chapultepec has many things to see. There is a hill in the middle of the park, and a castle was built on top of the hill. Later the castle was turned into a museum. People can see several famous murals there. They were painted by Diego Rivera and other famous artists. People can also see the Tlaloc fountain. It was designed by Rivera to look like an Aztec god of water. There are other museums and a zoo in the park.

Chapultepec is a beautiful park where visitors can learn about the different aspects of Mexican culture.

2 **GROUP WORK** Share your posters or brochures with three or four other students. Ask and answer questions about the different places.

UNIT 4

1 Read this message on social media. Then write an update about your life since high school for the newsletter. Include the following information:

- your name and when you attended your high school
- what you were like in high school

- what you are like now
- what you are doing

CALLING ALL SPU TIGERS! *IT'S NEWSLETTER TIME!*

We can't have a high school reunion every year, but we can keep the Tiger spirit with updates on our graduates. This month our update is from Tomoki Sawyer. You can send your own update to editor@SPUtiger987.net.

Hello Tigers!

I was a student at SPU from 2011–2015. Maybe you won't remember me. I was the kind of kid who went to the robotics lab at lunchtime. I was very reserved. After I graduated, I moved to Pittsburg and studied computer science at Carnegie Mellon University. Now I am more outgoing and adventurous. In fact, I'm moving to Yokohama, Japan to work for a company that makes robots!

I'd love to hear from my old friends. Please message me when you have the chance!

2 **PAIR WORK** Take turns reading your updates. Then write a response to your partner.

UNIT 5

1 Read the online product review. Then write a review of a product you bought recently. Answer these questions in your review:

- What is the product? Why did you buy it?
- How does it look and how well does it work?
- Would you recommend it? What is the best feature? Are there any problems?

🏠   Search 🔍   ⊗ Profile

Burst Home Security Guard ◉◉◉◉○

The Burst Home Security Guard is a smart robotic device that protects your home. As I travel a lot for work and I'm often away from home, I really needed some sort of home security system. But I didn't want to spend a lot of money so this little guard looked perfect for me!

This robot on wheels is about a foot tall and has a camera. It was fairly easy to setup and I did it in about 30 minutes with the help of the training video online.

Now when I leave the house, I just push a button on my phone, and it's set. The only downside is that the battery only lasts about 72 hours, which can be a problem when I am traveling.

2 PAIR WORK Compare your reviews. Decide how many stars to give each product.

UNIT 6

1 Read the first part of a short story. Then imagine how it might end and write the rest of the story. Answer these questions:

- How did Ava know Mike's name?
- Who is she hiding from?
- What does Mike do?
- What happens as a result of his decision?

The **Mysterious** Traveler

Mike hadn't expected trouble, but trouble came anyway. He had just checked into his ocean-view room at the hotel, and he was about to take a nap when there was a knock on the door.

"Who is it?" Mike called from the bed.

"Ava! Hurry, let me in!"

Mike had never met anyone named Ava, at least not that he could remember. He reluctantly got up. Whoever it was, kept knocking. When he opened the door, Mike was a little angry.

A tall woman pushed by him and walked into the room.

"You've got to hide me," she said.

"I don't even know you!" said Mike.

"Yes, you do!" she said looking at him with desperation in her eyes. "And you are the only one who can help me!"

2 GROUP WORK Compare your endings. How are your stories different?

UNIT 7

1 Read this online conversation. Then write a conversation about real or imaginary things you've done to change your appearance.

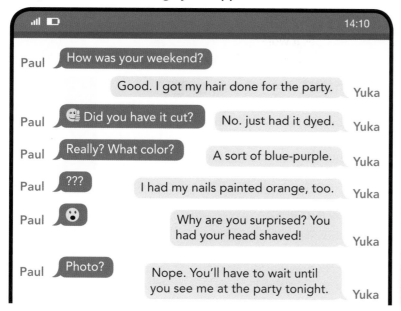

14:10

Paul: How was your weekend?

Yuka: Good. I got my hair done for the party.

Paul: 😕 Did you have it cut?

Yuka: No. just had it dyed.

Paul: Really? What color?

Yuka: A sort of blue-purple.

Paul: ???

Yuka: I had my nails painted orange, too.

Paul: 😮

Yuka: Why are you surprised? You had your head shaved!

Paul: Photo?

Yuka: Nope. You'll have to wait until you see me at the party tonight.

2 PAIR WORK Compare your conversations. Ask your partner follow-up questions.

UNIT 8

1 Read this letter to the editor of the local newspaper about a neighborhood project. Then write your own letter about a project you would like to start in your neighborhood. Describe the project, why you want to do it, and how people can be involved.

THE SUNSET HEIGHTS WEEKLY
Serving the Sunset Heights Community since 1927

Dear Neighbors,

Sunset Heights is a great place to live. My husband and I love the neighborhood and the people. However, we have one small problem. We love gardening, but we live in an apartment, so we do not have a place to grow anything. Then we heard about the city's community gardens project. We thought Sunset Heights would be perfect if we had one. We started looking for a location. Last week we got good news: the city has agreed to let us use the empty lot on 24th and Aurora Street! Now we'd like to invite the community to a planning meeting. If you'd like to join us, please meet at 926 Aurora Street at, 10 a.m. (No need to bring your gardening tools… yet!)

Hope to see you there,

Maria and Marcos Hernandez

2 PAIR WORK Compare your letters. Which projects will make the neighborhood safer? Which one will make it more attractive? Which will make it friendlier?

UNIT 9

1 Read these question-and-answer posts on an international student message board.
Then write your own post about a situation that went wrong and ask for advice.

Wall   Friends   Profile @

Making a good impression

I am an international college student, and I'm having a lot of new experiences. Most of them are good, but I've made some mistakes. I had dinner with my American roommate's family last month and I was so nervous I couldn't speak. I know I should have talked more, but they were speaking quickly, laughing and joking. I just sat there and smiled. What would you have done in that situation? I know it's going to happen again, and I want to be ready.   *K.L.*

PREPARE!

I have a tip: read something or watch a show in English and practice talking about that topic before you go.   *Loreta C.*

SHOW INTEREST

It sounds like a fun family! I would have just listened, too. But that's okay—most people love a good listener!   *Juan*

TELL THE TRUTH

Don't worry! Just say you are nervous. They'll understand and when you are ready, you can join in.   *Ping*

 2   GROUP WORK Compare your posts. Give your partners advice and then listen to their advice for you. Which advice is the most useful?

UNIT 10

1 Read the news article. Then imagine you were one of the witnesses and write an email to the news site. Include the following information:

- where you were, what you were doing, and who you were with
- what you saw and how you felt
- what you think the lights might have been

STRANGE LIGHTS IN THE NIGHT SKY

Last week, Louise Tucker was taking her dog for a late-night walk when she noticed a set of strange lights in the sky. "They were very bright lights," she said. "At first I thought they were bolts of lightning from a distant storm, but then I realized they were moving very fast." Scared, Tucker hurried home to get her camera and her husband. The two rushed out and managed to take a video before the lights disappeared.

The Tuckers thought they might have seen a group of planes, but after they spoke to their neighbors, who also saw the lights, the Tuckers took the video to the police. Chief of police Mark O'Reilly said that they are looking into the incident, but claimed that they have no idea what the lights were.

If you think you might have seen anything, please send in your story.

 2   PAIR WORK Compare your emails. Whose explanation is the most creative? Whose is the most believable?

UNIT 11

1 Read the text about the first X-ray. Then write a description of an invention you know about. Try to include the following information:

- when it was invented
- who invented it
- why it was invented
- how things would be different without the invention

HOW THE X-RAY WAS INVENTED

A German scientist named Wilhelm Röntgen invented the X-ray in 1895 by accident. At first, he was doing experiments to see if cathode rays could pass through glass. As he was working in his lab, he noticed a green light on a screen. He looked at his equipment: his cathode ray tubes were covered in black paper but somehow the rays were passing through the paper. Röntgen was surprised and curious. He named his invention the X-ray, and he decided to do more experiments. One day, he took an X-ray picture of his wife's hand. He was amazed when he saw a clear view of her bones. His wife was not so happy. "I have seen my death," she said. However, X-ray technology turned out to be a life-saving medical invention. If the X-ray had not been invented, doctors would not have had a way to see broken bones, cancer, or other problems inside the body.

2 Compare your descriptions. Ask your partner follow-up questions.

UNIT 12

1 Read the news article by a local journalist. Then imagine you are a journalist and write your own story about one of the following in your community:

- a new business that has opened.
- a sports event, a concert, or a performance.
- a change to roads or public buildings.
- someone who has won an award, achieved a goal, or done something special.

Home | News | Sports | Weather | Video

Soccer Team Breaks Record

The North Town Wolves have done it again! The high school soccer team will compete at the state championship for the fifth year in a row. Last night the Wolves beat the Evergreen Flying Falcons in overtime. The Wolves' team captain, Daewon Lee, scored the winning goal with a head shot that went straight into the net. After the game, coach Remi Mitchell, said that Lee had not been playing well due to an injured knee, so he had almost kept him out of the  game. "I'm glad I didn't!" he said. When asked about the goal, Lee said that he had simply been in the right place at the right time. The Wolves will be heading to the state championship on November 5.

2 **PAIR WORK** Share your articles. Which article is the most surprising, the most exciting, or the most unusual?

UNIT 1

The present perfect continuous; *since* and *for*

We use the present perfect continuous to talk about something that happens repeatedly or continuously from a time in the past until now.

- *How long **have** you **been studying**?* (= continuously up to now)
- *He **has been talking** on the phone for an hour.* (= continuously for the past hour)
- ***Have** you **been taking** tennis lessons for very long?* (= repeatedly up to now)

Notice the difference between the present perfect and the present perfect continuous. We use the present perfect to talk about experiences. We use the present perfect continuous to emphasize that something happened continuously or repeatedly.

- *I**'ve watched** that movie three times.* (= the whole movie three times at some point in the past)
- *I**'ve been watching** this movie for the past hour.* (= continuously for the past hour)
- *Somebody **has used** my camera.* (= at least one time and in the recent past)
- *Somebody **has been using** my camera.* (= repeatedly)

We form the present perfect continuous with *have* or *has* + *been* + present participle (*-ing* form)

Statements					
I / You / We / They	**have** **'ve** **have not** **haven't**	**been running.**	He / She / It	**has** **'s** **has not** **hasn't**	**been running.**

We often use the present perfect continuous with *since* + a date or time and *for* + a period of time.

- *I have been running marathons **since 2019**.* (~~I have been running marathons for 2019.~~)
- *I have been running marathons **for two years**.* (~~I have been running marathons since two years.~~)

NOW PRACTICE

1 Rewrite the questions using *how long* and the present perfect continuous.

1. When did you start doing yoga?

   How long have you been doing yoga ?

2. When did he start playing the violin?

   _____ ?

3. When did they begin doing volunteer work?

   _____ ?

4. When did you start taking dance lessons?

   _____ ?

2 Complete the sentences with *since* or *for*.

1. She's been playing the violin ____since____ she was a child.

2. I can't believe it. We've been talking on the phone _____ more than an hour!

3. Where have you been? I've been waiting for you _____ noon.

4. He's been playing the same song _____ the last hour. I'm getting tired of it.

UNIT 2
Indirect questions
We use indirect questions to make a question more polite or more formal.

Wh- questions
- *Can you tell me **what happened in class today?*** (= What happened in class today?)
- *Do you know **why this show is popular?*** (= Why is this show popular?)

Yes / No questions
- *Can you tell me **if we won the game?*** (= Did we win the game?)
- *Do you know **if the bookstore is open tonight?*** (= Is the bookstore open tonight?)

In indirect questions, the verb follows the subject, as in a statement. We do not use a helping verb unless it is a negative question.

- *What **is** his name?* → *What do you think his name **is**? (What do you think is his name?)*
- *Why **did** he **leave?*** → *Can you explain why he **left**? (Can you explain why did he leave?)*
- *Why **didn't** he **stay?*** → *I wonder why he **didn't stay**. (I wonder why didn't he stay.)*
- *Why **didn't** he **text?*** → *Do you know why he **didn't text**? (Do you know why didn't he text?)*

NOW PRACTICE

1 Rewrite the indirect questions as direct questions.

1. Can you explain why people watch so much TV?
   Why do people watch so much TV ?

2. Do you know why reality shows are so popular?
   _____ ?

3. Do you know who Chris Hemsworth is?
   _____ ?

4. Can you tell me when they made that movie?
   _____ ?

5. I wonder if this is a cooking show.
   _____ ?

2 Rewrite the direct questions as indirect questions.

1. What is the most popular video game?
   Do you know _what the most popular video game is_ ?

2. Are travel shows more popular than game shows?
   I wonder if _____ .

3. Why is this band so popular?
   Can you explain _____ ?

4. Who won the award for best actor?
   Can you tell me _____ ?

5. Why don't people watch more documentaries?
   Do you know _____ ?

UNIT 3

Passives

In an active sentence, the subject is the performer of the action. In a passive sentence, the subject is the receiver of the action.

Active sentence	Passive sentence
Eiffel designed the Statue of Liberty. (Eiffel = the performer of the action)	**The Statue of Liberty** was designed by Eiffel. (the Statue of Liberty = the receiver of the action)
My father wrote this book. (my father = the performer of the action)	**This book** was written by my father. (this book = the receiver of the action)

We often use the passive when the performer of the action (the agent) is unknown, obvious from the context, or when the agent refers to people in general.

- *My car **was stolen.*** (by an unknown person)
- *Our food was cold when it **was served.*** (by a waiter. This is obvious from the context.)
- *What **is** this **called** in English?* (by people in general)

In simple present and simple past statements, we form the passive with a helping verb + past participle. The verb agrees with the subject of the passive sentence.

Statements: simple present			
I	**am (not)**		
You / We / They	**are (not)**	**admired**	by fans.
He / She / It	**is (not)**		

Statements: simple past			
I / He / She / It	**was (not)**	**admired**	by fans.
He / She / It	**were (not)**		

NOW PRACTICE

1 Complete the sentences with the passive form of the verb in parentheses.

1. Central Park is my favorite place in New York. It ____is visited____ by millions of people every year. (visit)

2. The Marina Bay Sands resort in Singapore _____ by Moshe Safdie. (design)

3. Leonardo da Vinci _____ by many of the painters of his time. (admire)

4. We finished the tour by noon, but we _____ to stay for a presentation afterward. (invite)

5. This photo _____ when I was eight years old. (take)

2 Complete the statements with the passive form of a verb in the box.

complete	paint	name	locate

1. The Eiffel Tower _____is located_____ next to the river Seine in Paris.

2. This landmark _____ after the engineer Gustave Eiffel.

3. It _____ in 1889.

4. It _____ every seven years.

UNIT 4

Relative clauses (subject and object)

We can use a relative clause to identify, define, or classify a person or thing. The relative clause follows a noun.

- *I have a lot of friends **who are interested in music.***
- *I work in a store **which sells musical instruments.***

We can begin a relative clause with the relative pronoun *who, which,* or *that.* We use *who* for people, *which* for things, and *that* for people or things.

- *I have a <u>friend</u> **who** is very generous.*
- *I go to a <u>school</u> **which** is very traditional.*
- *Do you like <u>people</u> **that** talk a lot?*
- *Can you find a <u>video</u> **that** will make me laugh?*

The relative pronouns *who, which,* and *that* can function as the subject or object of the relative clause.

Relative pronoun as subject (noun + subject relative pronoun + <u>verb</u>)	Relative pronoun as object (noun + object relative pronoun + <u>noun / pronoun</u>+ verb)
I like a <u>game</u> **that** <u>is</u> challenging.	I saw a <u>movie</u> **that** I liked.
I like to be around <u>people</u> **who** <u>are</u> friendly.	Those are the <u>people</u> **who** <u>she</u> likes.

When the relative pronoun is the subject of the relative clause, the verb agrees with the noun that comes before it. When the relative pronoun is the object, the verb agrees with the subject of the relative clause.

- *I know lots of <u>people</u> who **are** outgoing. (I know lots of people who is outgoing.)*
- *Those are the people who <u>he</u> **was talking** about. (Those are the people who he were talking about.)*

We can also begin a relative clause with the possessive relative pronoun *whose. Whose* indicates that the noun that follows it belongs to the preceding noun.

- *These are the <u>people</u> **whose** party was last week.*
- *This is the <u>woman</u> **whose** children study with me.*
- *These are the <u>people</u> **whose** house she rents.*
- *This is the <u>man</u> **whose** sister you hired.*

We can omit *who, which,* and *that* in object relative clauses, but we can never omit *whose.*

- *This is the guy **they introduced me to.***
- *I loved the movie **we watched last night.***
- *This is the boy **whose parents I met yesterday.** (This is the boy parents I met yesterday.)*

NOW PRACTICE

1 Complete the sentences with the relative pronouns *who, which,* or *that.*

1. I have a friend <u>who / that</u> I always visit on Saturday.

2. She has an unusual name _____ I always forget.

3. My friends and I play a computer game _____ is really popular.

4. I'd like to meet someone _____ doesn't talk a lot.

2 Complete the sentences. Use the correct form of the verb in parentheses.

1. There isn't anyone here that he ___<u>wants</u>___ to meet. (want)

2. This museum has a modern art display that you _____ to see before it closes. (need)

3. Did you invite anyone who he _____ ? (know)

4. I've never met the girls who _____ that song, but I'd like to! (sing)

UNIT 5

Infinitives and gerunds (for purpose)

When we want to talk about the general purpose or use of something, we can use an infinitive or *for* + gerund.

- *I often use my phone (**in order**) **to share** photos.*
- *I often use my phone **for sharing** photos.*

Infinitive	
I use this app This app can be used I downloaded this app	**(in order) to send** messages.

Gerund	
I use this app This this app can be used I downloaded this app	**for sending** messages.

We can also use an infinitive (but not a gerund) to talk about someone's purpose or reason for doing something.

- *I went to the camera store (**in order**) **to buy** a new camera.*
- *(I went to the camera store for buying a new camera.)*

The expression *in order to* is slightly more formal than *to*. *In order not to* is more common than *in order to*.

- *You must have a passport **in order to go** overseas.*
- *We entered the room quietly **in order not to disturb** anyone.*
- *She invited everyone to the party **in order not to insult** anyone.*

NOW PRACTICE

1 **Where possible, rewrite each sentence using a gerund.**

1. We can't use a dictionary to look up words during a test.

   We can't use a dictionary for looking up words during a test .

2. You can borrow my tablet to do your homework.

   _____ .

3. Did you use a spell checker to find mistakes in your paper?

   _____ ?

4. Do you use wireless headphones to listen to podcasts?

   _____ ?

5. Did you buy that fitness app to use when you go running?

   _____ ?

6. Do you know anyone who doesn't use email to communicate?

   _____ ?

7. I called my mom to tell her I'll be late.

   _____ .

8. He wants a better camera to make videos.

   _____ .

UNIT 6

The past perfect

We use the past perfect to show that one event in the past took place before another past event. The past perfect signals the earlier event. The simple past signals the later event.

• *When we <u>arrived</u>, the party **had** already **started**.* (= First the party started and then we arrived.)
• *She **had** already **left** when I <u>called</u>.* (= First she left and then I called.)
• *We just <u>learned</u> that she **had had** a child.* (= She had the child first and then we learned about it.)

We form the past perfect with *had* + past participle.

Statements		
I / You / He / She / It / We / They	**had left**	by the time I got there.
I / You / He / She / It / We / They	**had not left** **hadn't left**	by the time I got there.

We often use the past perfect in sentences with *because* or *when*.

• *She was upset <u>because</u> she **had missed** her flight.*
• *She was late to the airport <u>because</u> she **had forgotten** to set her alarm.*
• *<u>When</u> she got to the airport, the plane **had** already **taken off**.*
• *I **had** just **fallen** asleep <u>when</u> the phone rang.*

We often use the past perfect in sentences with *by the time* + a simple past verb.

• *<u>By the time</u> I was 21, **I had traveled** all over the world.*
• *She **had** already **left** <u>by the time</u> I got there.*

The words *before* and *after* can also make the order of events clear. When we use these words, the past perfect is not required.

• *They arrived a few minutes <u>after</u> we left.*
• *We ate dinner <u>before</u> they arrived.*

NOW PRACTICE

1 **Complete the sentences with the simple past or past perfect form of the verb in parentheses.**

1. By the time he _____was_____ 19, he had already graduated from college. (be)

2. I _____ to Asia for the first time when I was 22. (go)

3. We couldn't find the keys because my brother _____ them in the car. (leave)

4. By the time we got to the beach, it _____ to rain. (start)

5. When I got to school, I discovered that I _____ my glasses. (forget)

6. We were tired because we _____ hard all day. (work)

7. I couldn't sleep last night because I _____ too much coffee. (drink)

8. I _____ a chance to say goodbye because he had already left. (not have)

9. When he realized his exam was the next day, James _____ very hard. (study)

10. Before she _____ shopping, Carol made a list. (go)

UNIT 7

Have / get something done

We use *have / get* + object + past participle when we ask someone else to do something for us.

- *I'm going to **have my hair cut**.* (= Someone else is going to cut my hair.)
- *She **got her nails done**.* (= Someone else did her nails.)

In the structure *have / get* + object + past participle, *have* and *get* function as main verbs.

Subject	have / get	Object	past participle
I	have	my car	washed.
You	get	your hair	dyed.
He	has	his house	painted.
She	gets	her computer	fixed.

The object always comes between the main verb (*have / get*) and the past participle.

- *She is going to have **her hair** dyed.* (~~She is going to have dyed her hair.~~)

We can use *have / get* + object + past participle to talk about events in the present, past, and future.

- *I **have** my hair **cut** every month.*
- *I'm **having** my nails **done**.*
- *I've **had** my hair **dyed** several times.*
- *I **got** my car **washed** yesterday.*
- *I'm **going to get** my beard **trimmed**.*

- *Where **do** you **get** your hair **cut**?*
- *Why **are** you **having** your nails **done**?*
- ***Have** you ever **had** your hair **dyed**?*
- ***Did** you **get** the car **washed**?*
- ***Are** you **going to get** your beard **trimmed**?*

NOW PRACTICE

1 Rewrite the sentences. Use *have / get* + object + past participle in your new sentence.

1. I paid someone to fix my car.

   I had my car fixed .

2. I'm going to ask someone to check my homework.

   _____ .

3. I paid a hair stylist to dye my hair.

   _____ .

4. We've paid someone to clean our apartment several times.

   _____ .

5. I pay someone to edit my writing.

   _____ .

6. I've never asked someone to do my nails.

   _____ .

7. I asked the woman to deliver the flowers.

   _____ .

8. I haven't found someone to fix my bicycle.

   _____ .

UNIT 8

Second conditional

We use the second conditional to describe unlikely, impossible, or imaginary conditions and results in the present or future. The *if* clause introduces the imaginary condition. The main clause expresses the imaginary result.

- *If I had enough money, I'd buy a car.* (= I don't have enough money now, so I can't buy a car.)
- *If I exercised every day, I'd feel great.* (= I don't exercise every day, so I don't feel great.)

We use the past tense in the *if* clause and *would, could,* or *might* in the main clause. *Could* and *might* express less certainty than *would. Could* means "would be able to" and *might* means "would possibly."

- *If I **had** lots of friends, I **would be** happy.* (= I'm sure I would be happy.)
- *If I **had** lots of friends, I **could be** happy.* (= I would be able to be happy.)
- *If I **had** lots of friends, I **might be** happy.* (= It's possible I would be happy.)

We can use affirmative or negative verbs in either clause or in both clauses. We can also use the *if* clause at the beginning or end of the sentence. If it is first, we use a comma after it.

- *If my grades **were** better, my parents **would be** happy.*
- *I **wouldn't need** to study on the weekend if my grades **were** better.*
- *If I **didn't have** so much homework, I **wouldn't get up** so early.*

We use *were* in the *if* clause for the first and third person singular, but *was* is also common in informal conversation.

- *If I **were** rich, I'd buy an apartment in the city.* (= Informal: If I was rich, I'd buy an apartment in the city.)
- *If my bicycle **weren't** broken, I'd ride it to work.* (= Informal: If my bicycle wasn't broken, I'd ride it to work)

NOW PRACTICE

1 Rewrite the sentences using the second conditional.

1. I want to travel, but I don't have enough money.

   If I had enough money, I would travel.

2. I want to do something outdoors today, but I have to go to school.

   _____ .

3. She wants to be healthy, but she eats a lot of junk food.

   _____ .

4. I want to buy some flowers, but I don't have enough money.

   _____ .

5. He wants to go out tonight, but he's sick.

   _____ .

6. I want to help them, but I'm really tired.

   _____ .

7. They want to see each other, but they are too busy.

   _____ .

8. My parents want to move here, but the housing prices are too high.

   _____ .

UNIT 9

Should have and *would have*

We use *should have* and *would have* + past participle to talk about imagined situations in the past.
We use *should have* to express advice in the past (it implies the correct action was not done).
We use *would have* to suggest an alternative to the action taken.

- *You **should have sent** a birthday card.* (= You didn't send a card and that was a mistake.)
- *You **shouldn't have been** late.* (= You were late and that was a mistake.)
- *Why did you go to France? I **would have gone** to Italy.* (= In the same situation, I would have done something different.)

We often use questions with *should have* or *would have* to ask for advice about a past action.

Yes / No questions		
Should **Would**	I / you / he / she / it / we / they	**have waited**?

Wh- questions			
What	**should** **would**	I / you / he / she / it / we / they	**have done**?

NOW PRACTICE

1 **Read each sentence. Write a response using *should have* or *shouldn't have*.**

1. Margo drove very fast and got a speeding ticket.

   She _shouldn't have driven so fast_____ .

2. Andy didn't study for the test, and he got a very bad grade.

   He _____ .

3. Martin didn't apologize for being late.

   He _____ .

4. Her children didn't help cook dinner.

   They _____ .

2 **Read each sentence. Write a response using *would have* or *wouldn't have*.**

1. Why didn't Paula offer to help?

   I _would have offered to help_____ .

2. Why didn't Carl invite Sandra to the party?

   I _____ .

3. Why didn't Lester take a gift?

   I _____ .

4. Why did Angela talk to him?

   I _____ .

UNIT 10

May, might, could, and *must + have*

We use *may, might, could,* and *must + have* + past participle to talk about degrees of certainty in the past.

Degrees of certainty	
must have	almost 100% sure it was true
may (not) have	
might (not) have	not sure if it was true
could have	
must not have	almost 100% sure it was not true
couldn't have	

We use *must have* + past participle when we are almost certain that something was true in the past.

• *The street was wet when I got up. It **must have rained** last night.* (= I'm almost certain it rained.)

We use *must not have* and *couldn't have* + past participle when we are almost certain that something was <u>not</u> true in the past.

• *He doesn't have a passport. He **couldn't have left** the country.* (= I'm almost certain he <u>didn't</u> leave the country.)
• *The food is still on the table. They **must not have eaten**.* (= I'm almost certain they <u>didn't</u> eat.)

We use *may have, may not have, might have, might not have,* and *could have* + past participle when we are not sure what happened. We are just guessing.

• *I can't find my book. I **may have left** it at work.*
• *I heard a strange noise last night. It **might have been** the wind.*
• *Dora didn't go to the party. She **might not have gotten** an invitation.*
• *She saw a light in the distance. It **could have been** a fire.*

NOW PRACTICE

1 Rewrite the bold sentences. Use *may (not), might (not), must (not),* or *could (not) + have.*

1. You can't really get a signal in the mountains. **I'm almost certain that he didn't call.**
   <u>He couldn't have called</u> .

2. That photo didn't look real. **It's possible that it was a fake.**
   _____ .

3. The clock says 3 o'clock, but that's impossible. **I'm sure the clock stopped.**
   _____ .

4. I heard a loud noise during the night. **I'm guessing that it was an ambulance.**
   _____ .

5. There wasn't any food in the refrigerator. **I'm sure they didn't go to the grocery store.**
   _____ .

6. My brother hasn't gone to work all week. **I'm almost certain that he lost his job.**
   _____ .

UNIT 11

Third conditional

We use the third conditional to talk about unreal or imaginary conditions and results in the past. The *if* clause introduces the imaginary event or condition in the past. The main clause expresses the imaginary result.

- *If we had left on time, we wouldn't have been late.* (= We didn't leave on time, so we were late.)
- *If she had called, he wouldn't have gotten angry.* (= She didn't call, so he got angry.)

We use the past perfect in the *if* clause and a modal + *have* + past participle in the main clause. The *if* clause can come before or after the main clause. If it is first, we use a comma after it.

if + past perfect	modal + *have* + past participle
If he **had gone** to college,	he **would have become** an inventor.
If she **hadn't gone** to college,	she **would have worked** in the family business.
modal + *have* + past participle	***if* + past perfect**
I **would have gone** to Canada	if **I had gone** anywhere.
She **would have stayed** for dinner	if she **hadn't had** an appointment.

We can use affirmative or negative verbs in either clause or in both clauses.

- *If I **hadn't had** so much work, I **would have gone** to the movies last night.*
- *If my grades **had been** lower, I **wouldn't have gone** to college.*
- *If I **hadn't studied** computer science, I **wouldn't have learned** about app design.*

We often use the third conditional to ask imaginary or hypothetical questions.

Wh- questions
What **would** you **have studied** if you **had not chosen** your current major?
Where **would** you **have gone** if this university **hadn't accepted** you?
How **would** you **have gotten** there if your parents **hadn't taken** you?

NOW PRACTICE

1 **Complete the sentences. Use the correct form of the verb in parentheses.**

1. If I ___hadn't eaten___ already, I would have gone to lunch with them. (not / eat)

2. If we _____ you were in town, we would have asked you to dinner. (know)

3. If he had been wearing his seatbelt, he _____ a ticket. (not / get)

4. If she had told me the truth, I _____ . (understand)

5. What would you have done with your money if you _____ a house? (not / buy)

6. What would she have done if she _____ an inventor? (not / become)

7. Where would you have gone to college if you _____ into Harvard? (not / get)

8. If I had been born 100 years ago, I _____ a hard life. (have)

9. If they _____ the translation app, they would have understood the menu. (download)

10. How would we have met, if you _____ us? (not / introduce)

UNIT 12

Reported speech

Direct speech is the speaker's exact words. Reported speech is a restatement of the speaker's words.

Direct speech	Reported speech
"I'm in Venezuela," she said.	She said (that) she was in Venezuela.
She said, "I'm visiting my family."	She said (that) she was visiting her family.
She said, "Caracas is beautiful."	*She said (that) Caracas is beautiful.

When the reporting verb (*say, explain, tell*, etc.) is in the past tense, it is common to change the verb tense in the *that* clause. This helps us to understand the order of events.

*When the speaker wants to be clear that the information is a general truth or still relevant for the present, tense changes aren't needed, the verb can stay in the present.

- "I **don't feel** well," said Jon.   Jon said he **didn't feel** well. (simple present → simple past)
- "I**'ll call** tonight," Ann said.   Ann said she **would call** tonight. (will → would)
- "I **can't** go," said Ben.   Ben said he **couldn't go**. (can → could)
- "She **left** at ten," Tom said.   Tom said she **had left** at ten. (simple past → past perfect)
- "It's a great movie," Bo said.   Bo said it's a great movie. (simple present → simple present)

The verb *tell* must be followed by an object (noun or pronoun). The verb *say* is not followed by an object.

- She **told** me that she liked Bangkok. (~~She told that she liked Bangkok.~~)
- She **said** that she was happy. (~~She said me that she was happy.~~)

When we report someone's question, we use statement word order.

Direct speech	Reported speech
"**Are you** interested in politics?"	He asked her **if she was** interested in politics.
"**Do you believe** that article?"	She asked me **if I believed** that article.
"Where **are you**?"	They asked her where **she was**.
"When **did you start** to write?"	We asked him when **he had started** to write.
"What time **are they coming** back?"	I asked you what time **they were coming** back.

NOW PRACTICE

1   Rewrite the sentences using reported speech.

1. "I can't go today," he said.   *He said he couldn't go today* .
2. "I'll see you tomorrow," she said.   _____ .
3. "I saw her yesterday," he said.   _____ .
4. "We did some research," she said.   _____ .
5. "They didn't go," he said.   _____ .
6. "I was traveling," she said.   _____ .
7. "Who do you believe?" she asked.   _____ .
8. "Why did she hide the truth?" he asked.   _____ .
9. "We can't help you," they said.   _____ .
10. "Who was that man?" they asked.   _____ .

UNIT 1
LISTENING page 7

H=Host P=Paco K=Kristin

H Welcome to *People at Play*. This week we have been talking to people who have turned hobbies into careers. Let's meet today's guests.

P My name is Paco and I love photography and biking.

K Hi, My name is Kristin, and I'm a cosplay artist.

H Great to have you both. Paco, let's start with you. How did you turn your hobby into a way to make money?

P Well, it starts with my city. I'm lucky to be from Seattle, which has amazing views of water and mountains, great architecture, and cool little neighborhoods. I've been riding my bike there all my life, and one day, I was biking with my friend, and she kept stopping to take photos. That gave me an idea. I decided to offer biking tours with photography lessons to tourists.

H And how does that work?

P I take groups on bicycles to the best scenic spots. Then I give a little lesson. For example, how to take good photos of light coming through the trees. Then my students take photos. I've been doing this for three years now and it's going well. In fact, I had to hire another person. Her name is Brittany.

H That's awesome! Thanks, Paco. Now let's talk to Kristin. Kristin, give us some background. What exactly is cosplay?

K Good question! *Cosplay* combines the words *costume* and *play*. It's the activity of dressing up like a character in a video game or a superhero from a movie and then going to a convention or party in the costume.

H That sounds like fun.

K It is! I've been doing it ever since my dad took me to my first comic book convention. I saw all these magical creatures and characters, and I said, "Wow, I want to do that!"

H Interesting. So then you started making your own costumes?

K Yes, I found this great community of cosplay artists online. The Internet is so good for making connections. I found websites where people post their designs and costumes. That's what encouraged me to start making my costumes.

H OK! And how did you start making money?

K Well, after people saw the costumes I made, they started messaging me and asking me to make costumes for them. In the beginning, they mostly wanted copies, but lately, I've been working with individuals on original designs. Now I have my own website where I sell products and design services.

H So customers came to you? That's great, Kristin!

LISTENING PLUS page 7

H=Host K=Kenji

H And now, let's meet one more guest. This man runs the biggest martial arts studio in town. Welcome Kenji Thomas.

K Hello.

H So tell us the story. How did you find out you were good at this? Did you fight a lot? Do you have brothers?

K (*Laughs*) The truth is, I'm the oldest. My brothers are afraid of me! But seriously, karate has always been a big part of my life, but I thought it was just a hobby.

H What changed your mind?

K Honestly, it was a trip to Japan with my high school. We visited a dojo. That's a karate studio, and I learned about the art and discipline of the sport. I realized that karate is much more than physical exercise. It's about living a good and honorable life. Ever since then, it has been my dream to copy what I saw in Japan here.

H So you opened your own dojo in the States.

K That's right. I've been running this place for about five years now, and it's been a very rewarding experience.

H So do you have any advice for our listeners about turning a hobby into a business?

K That's a good question. I guess I'd say, you have to work hard and get really good at your hobby. You also need to be sure that it is something that other people want to learn. Do some market research! It's not enough to just like something, you have to have something special to offer people.

H That's great advice. Thanks for being on the show, Kenji.

K My pleasure.

UNIT 2
LISTENING page 13

1. B=Bill K=Kitty MV=Mrs. Vandervault

   B Welcome to the Island Hotel! Are you checking in?

   K Yes, my name is Kitty. Kitty Cooper.

   B Ah yes, we've been expecting you. My name is Bill Jones. I'm the head clerk here at the front desk. You are in room 305. You'll have a view of the beach.

   K Thank you, Bill. An ocean view is just what I need. I'm here to relax.

B Then you have come to the right place. It's very peaceful here. Just the sound of the ocean, and a gentle breeze.

K Fantastic, I think I'll unpack and then go for a walk by the water.

B That's a great way to relax after a long flight.

MV Help! Help! Police!

B Mrs. Vandervault, what's the matter? Let me help. Can you tell me what happened?

MV There's been a robbery! Someone has stolen my jewelry. It's worth thousands. Hurry. Call the police!

2. K=Kitty   I=Inspector

K Good morning, I'm Kitty Cooper. You wanted to talk to me?

I Hello, Ms Cooper, I'm Inspector David Truelock of the Island police department. Thank you for agreeing to answer some questions.

K Is this about the missing jewelry?

I If you don't mind, I'll ask the questions. Can you tell me what you did yesterday?

K I flew in from New York and took a taxi here. Then as I was checking in, Mrs. Vandervault came rushing in and said her jewelry was gone.

I And after that?

K Well, after you and the other police arrived, I went for a walk along the beach to calm down.

I Did you see anything unusual?

K There was a couple arguing.

I Oh? Could you hear what they said?

K No, I was too far from them and I couldn't hear them over the sound of the ocean. The man was behind a palm tree. But I got a good look at the woman, and she had purple hair.

I Purple hair?

K Yes.

I Okay. Thank you for your time.

K You are welcome. Please let me know if there is anything else I can do. I'm a detective in New York.

I Ahhh, I should have known. Thank you for telling me, but this is not New York City, Ms. Cooper. Just relax and enjoy your vacation.

3. K Good morning, Inspector.

I Well, well, if it isn't Detective Cooper from New York City. Come in!

K I wanted to know if you had made any progress in finding the jewelry.

I This is just the beginning of our investigation.

K Well, I might have a clue.

I If you know something, then tell me.

K I found this ring on the beach this morning, right near where the couple were arguing.

I Wow! That is a very large diamond! I wonder if it's real.

K It could be, Inspector. Do you know if it belongs to Mrs. Vandervault?

I Thank you for turning it in, Ms. Cooper. Now may I suggest you try the Sunset Cafe for breakfast. If you hurry, you can get a table by the window. And, please, stay out of the investigation.

LISTENING PLUS page 13

I You again?

K Good morning, Inspector. I have some information.

I Is that so? What?

K I think Bill the hotel clerk is the man I saw at the beach last night. The one arguing with the young woman.

I And why do you say that? He's about to become my son-in-law.

K Oh, I see. He's marrying your daughter? How nice!

I I don't know why I told you that. Now tell me why you think he's involved.

K There was purple hair on his shirt.

I That doesn't mean anything.

K Does your daughter have purple hair, Inspector?

I That's personal.

K Is that a photo of your daughter on your desk, Inspector? She has purple hair …

I Yes, my daughter has purple hair but that doesn't mean anything.

K I think you are trying to protect your daughter. The clerk stole the jewelry, and he wanted your daughter to hide it. That explains the arguing. I think she told you, and you are trying to help her.

I But it will break her heart. . . she's my only child.

K Inspector, you must do your job and arrest that man. You don't want a thief for a son-in-law!

UNIT 3

LISTENING page 19

1. Welcome to The Hakone Open Air Museum. The museum was opened in 1969, and it is still one of the few open-air museums in Japan. It was designed to show sculpture in a beautiful outdoor setting. Today you will see works by important artists from Japan and around the world.
    As you walk through the garden, notice that you can move all the way around the art and how the hills and forests that surround the sculptures affect your experience. What makes this museum unique is the way the seasons change the sculptures.

As you go around the corner to exhibit one, you will see a figure face down in the grass. Think about how the grass changes your feelings about the figure. Perhaps it looks cool and peaceful to you on a summer day. Imagine how different it might look in winter when the figure is lying face down in the snow.

The art here is child friendly. If you are with children, make a stop at the *Woods of Net*. This sculpture is for all ages, but as you enter the sculpture, you will see colorful hanging nets and happy children climbing in them!

2. Your tour starts outside the Museum of Pop Culture. This unique building is a great place to learn about modern architecture, rock music, science fiction, and technology.

Let's start outside the building. Here in the northwestern corner of the United States, the seasons change often and so does the position of the sun. See that bright pink color in the morning light? In the afternoon, it may change to purple. The architect Frank O. Gehry did this on purpose. He wanted to capture the energy and wildness of rock and roll music. Notice those curved walls, they are meant to remind you of an electric guitar.

As you go inside, you enter the most important part of the museum called the *Sky Church*. It's an enormous space with a huge LED screen and it's the center of activity. Here you can watch films of historical concerts to get yourself in the mood to learn more about pop culture.

In the next room, notice a giant spiraling tower made of more than 500 guitars. It is about two stories tall and it looks as if a tornado is pulling the instruments up into the air.

Move through the exhibit to …

3. **G**=Guide **W**=Woman **T**=Teenager

G Welcome to the National Museum of Anthropology. This is the largest and most visited museum in Mexico. It is special because it has the biggest collection of art and history from pre-Hispanic times. Everything you will see today comes from the time before the Europeans arrived.

W When was that?

G The first Europeans came in the 16th century. Before their arrival, people had been developing art, science, and culture for more than 10,000 years.

W Wow, that's a long time. What kind of science?

G They studied the stars, and they were good at math. In fact, we'll see the famous Aztec Calendar today. It is more accurate than the modern calendar, yet it was made 600 years ago.

W And art?

G Follow me and I'll show you some. We are going to start with these giant stone heads. They were made by the Olmec people two to three thousand years ago. Most of the heads are taller than a human and can weigh about 40,000 kilograms.

T Wow! That's heavy.

G Yes. And we still aren't exactly sure how they moved them.

LISTENING PLUS page 19

J=James   L=Lisa

J Hello. Did I hear you say you just got back from Brazil?

L That's right. I work for an arts organization, and sometimes I get to travel for work. This was my first trip to Brazil.

J I'd love to go to Brazil. My name is James, by the way. I work with Dolores.

L Nice to meet you, James. I'm Lisa! I know Dolores from school. She's put on another great party, hasn't she?

J Yes, she has! So going back to your trip: did you visit art galleries and museums in Brazil? Any good ones?

L Well, it depends on what you are looking for. I am attracted to Brazilian work, so I started at Pinacoteca in São Paulo. It's smaller than the main art museum there, but it supports Brazilian artists.

J Did you like it?

L Very much. It's in a beautiful old building with lots of light, and they had an exhibit by Ernesto Neto. He makes unusual abstract installations. They really affected me.

J Really? How?

L Well, they are designed to make people think differently about space. Some shapes hang from the ceiling and others sort of grow up from the floor. It's hard to describe, but he definitely plays with reality.

J Cool. So, did you get to Rio de Jainero?

L Oh yes. There's lots to see there, especially the street art. I wanted to see Eduardo Kobra's work.

J Is he a street artist?

L Yes, one of many! Here, let me show you a photo.

J Wow, that's huge. It covers the whole block! And so many bright colors.

L That mural was designed by Kobra. I think maybe he got some help with the actual painting.

J Wow, you know a lot about Brazilian art.

L Not as much as I would like. I'm hoping to bring some Brazilian artists here for a group show.

J Wow! When you do, I'd like to come see it. You've made me curious.

UNIT 4

LISTENING page 27

1. I=Ivy   J=Jane

   I Jane! It's so good to see you! You look great! Here, let me take your suitcase.

   J Thanks. I can't believe we haven't seen each other since high school. We really shouldn't have waited this long.

   I I know. It's been ten years!

   J Seems like yesterday. I can still remember when we first met.

   I Me too. It was in the robotics club. You were the only other girl there!

   J Oh yeah. I don't know what I was thinking, but then I saw you, and I knew it was going to be okay.

   I Yeah, there weren't many girls who were into robotics back then.

   J We were such nerds.

   I We still are! And it turned out so well. I hear you're working for a start-up now.

   J Yes, I am and I'm definitely still a nerd and having a great time.

   I That's fantastic. Me too! I think we need to get together more often! Good thing we have some time to catch up before the reunion.

2. J=Jade   T=Trey

   J I'm nervous about your high school reunion. What will I say to your friends?

   T Don't worry. There's only one person who I really want you to meet, and that's Curtis.

   J Curtis? The one you call crazy Curtis?

   T That's the one. He's the guy who changed my life.

   J How did he do that?

   T Well, I used to be super insecure. I was too shy to talk to anyone or look them in the eye. So my mom got me a job as a camp counselor. I guess she thought it would be good for me, but I did not want to go.

   J Knowing your mom she made you go, right?

   T Right. So about five minutes after I got there, this guy came up to me and started asking me questions. Well, one thing led to another, and that night, when everyone else was sleeping, we snuck out of our cabin and went swimming! I never would have done that without Curtis!

   J Is he still like that?

   T I don't know. That's why I'm anxious to see him. I want to find out if he's still adventurous, or if he's changed into a regular person.

3. B=Beth   L=Louise

   B Mommy, how did you meet Daddy?

   L I met him in high school.

   B Tell me exactly what happened? Was it love at first sight?

   L No, not exactly.

   B Well, how did you meet him?

   L Okay, well, one morning, I was riding my bicycle to high school like usual but it was raining really hard so I was getting wet. I'd stopped at a red light and I was waiting for the light to change because I'm careful. You know that, Beth. We always wait for the light to turn green before we go.

   B Right, mommy.

   L So when it did turn green, I started to turn into the school parking lot when all of a sudden, I heard someone call my name, "Louise," I turned around, and pow! This guy on a skateboard crashed right into me and knocked me down.

   B Oh no! Was that Daddy?

   L That was your daddy. And the thing is, he didn't even fall off his skateboard!

   B He didn't?

   L No, but he did stop to see if I was okay. I was pretty upset. I was wet and covered in dirt, and I must have looked terrible. But he was so sorry, and the way he smiled at me, I just couldn't get mad.

   B That sounds like love at first sight, Mommy.

   L Well, maybe you're right, honey. It took about 30 seconds, so I guess it was.

LISTENING PLUS page 27

J=Jane   L=Louise

   J Hi Louise, do you remember me? We met senior year... when we worked on the yearbook together.

   L Oh sure, Jane Simmons. That was fun. I always admired you. You were into robotics, and you didn't care what anyone thought.

   J Oh I did, but I hid it well. Actually, I admired you! You always seemed so calm.

   L Ha, well you should see me now that I have kids!

   J I'm sure you're a fantastic mother. Hey, is that Curtis over there in the crowd?

   L Yes, it is. I guess you haven't seen him since high school. Does he look different to you?

   J Well, yeah. He used to have long hair, and he was super skinny. I remember he was always riding his skateboard. I didn't know him very well, but I always wondered what happened to him.

   L He's a dentist now.

   J A dentist? I never thought crazy Curtis was the kind of guy who would become a dentist. I thought he'd be a race car driver or something.

   L Well, I'm sure there are days when he wishes that.

   J So do you see him often?

   L Pretty often. He's my husband!

UNIT 5

LISTENING page 33

C=Chuck   M=Marci

C Welcome to the *App Round Up* where we review the latest apps. Summer is nearly here and a lot of you will be thinking about traveling so my co-host Marci DeLaurenti has been testing travel apps, and she wants to share her favorites.

M That's right, Chuck.

C Marci, what are some apps that you've downloaded to your personal device?

M I have three today, Chuck. The first is a free app called Bed.

C Bed? Just bed? Like you sleep in it?

M That's right. But not just any bed. This app finds historic or unusual hotels all around the world. For example, there are floating hotels on rivers, and once I stayed at a hotel that used to be a factory. It's fun to browse even when you aren't traveling!

C What is the most interesting place you've ever stayed?

M A treehouse hotel! I woke up with a group of monkeys outside my window.

C Sounds noisy!

M My next app is called CamTrans.

C What does that mean?

M It's a camera, cam, and a translator, trans. Put them together and you have Camtrans. Basically, it's a translation app, which is, of course, very useful for doing international business. Camtrans has some useful features. For example, you can point your camera at a sign or word, and it will give you a simple translation on your screen. I sometimes have to try several times in order to get the right phrase, but I expect the app to get better with time.

C Is it free?

M No. Camtrans costs $10.00, which is a lot for an app, but it's worth it, even if you're just going to use it for checking into a hotel on a family vacation.

C And your third app?

M My third app is for getting cheap tickets. It's called Tisket.

C Like Tickets?

M Yes, but with a s instead of a c in the middle. I love Tisket because I can find discount tickets on shows, concerts, and even tours.

C But don't other apps do that?

M Yes, but Tisket is super easy to use. The one problem with the app, is that the tickets only become available six hours before the performance. So you have to wait until that day's tickets are released before you can pick a show or concert from the list.

C Isn't that what traveling is all about? Trying something new at the last minute!

LISTENING PLUS page 33

C=Chuck   E=Ella   R=Raj   B=Barbara   M=Marci

C For our next section we asked listeners to share their favorite travel apps, and we got some interesting recommendations that we didn't know about. The first one comes from a travel writer, we also heard from a college student, and a retired couple.

E My name is Ella. Tripper is an app that can combine all my travel plans in one place. I just upload my ticket and reservation info, and it keeps everything in one place. It even sends me a message if my flight is delayed!

R Hello, my name is Raj, and my favorite app is Local Buddy. It matches travelers with local people who want to meet up for a meal or a tour. There's no fee involved, and it's a great way to find out about the place you're visiting from a local.

C And finally we heard from a woman who lives in a motor home.

B My name is Barbara. My husband and I made an app called Wandering. It's for people who live in vans and motor homes. The app helps us share information with other full-time travelers. We can post news and updates, ask and answer questions, and write reviews.

C So modern technology doesn't always separate people. In fact, the little buttons on our phones can connect us with experiences and people across time and distance.

M You are so right, Chuck. Thanks Ella, Raj, and Barbara for your recommendations. Now if you liked this episode of App Round Up, please like and share with your friends.

C Till next time!

UNIT 6

LISTENING page 39

N=Narrator

Chapter 9: Death Valley

N Cici and Liam were five hours out of Los Angeles, when the engine's fan belt broke. It happened just like that. One minute they were driving in a straight line through the desert, drinking coffee, and planning their next photo shoot for the Road Trip mini-series. The next minute, they were sitting in the shade of their small SUV, trying to find a signal.

"Are you sure we can't drive the car?" asked Cici.

"I'm sure," said Liam.

"What if no one comes?" asked Cici.

"Don't talk like that," said Liam. "This is a major highway. Someone has to come."

Cici didn't quite believe him. They had hardly seen any cars since turning onto this road. She looked up at the dry brown hills. Death Valley was a good name for this place, she thought. There were no trees, no plants, nothing; just hills, rocks, and dirt. And it was hot. Scary hot.

"Did you know," said Liam, "that a person can go three weeks without food but if they don't get water, they can die in a couple of days?"

"Thanks for the information, Liam," Cici said.

"I'm just saying that we have to be smart. Don't get any ideas about going off in search of water."

"I won't."

"There's nothing out there, Cici."

"I know."

"Good because sometimes I feel like you are just a bit too adventurous!"

By evening, they had run out of water. Cici's skin was red, and her lips were cracked. She was thirsty beyond belief and her head hurt. They had seen one truck, and it had passed them without stopping. Perhaps the driver hadn't seen them sitting next to the car. Maybe he thought the car was empty.

Now, with night falling, the dry air was cooling. A light wind blew Liam's hair away from his face. He smiled at Cici and rubbed his eyes.

"I think I see a star," he said looking over her shoulder.

"You can make a wish," Cici smiled. She looked up to the east where night was starting to cover the hills and spread across the sky.

Liam closed his eyes and moved his lips. "We'll be fine now," he joked, "but we'd better get in the car. It's going to be a long, cold night!"

Cici was just about to get into the car when something caught her eye. She turned and looked. Sure enough a light was shining on one of the hills. Was help nearby?

LISTENING PLUS page 39

N=Narrator

Chapter 10: Signs of life

N   At first, Liam didn't want to leave the safety of the car. "People travel on roads," he argued. "We aren't going to find help out there in the empty desert."

Cici was tired of waiting, however. She was too thirsty to sleep, and when a half-moon rose and shone a blue light across the desert floor, she finally convinced him that they could see well enough to travel.

"It's not as far as it looks," she said pointing at the light. "I promise. And we need water."

Liam shook his head. Finally, Cici suggested that an adventure would improve the show, and Liam reluctantly agreed to leave the safety of the car.

The pair walked silently, working their way across the desert floor and up the hill. Their eyes had adjusted to the night, and they could see every rock and branch in front of them. Soon they were close enough to see a campfire.

"I think it's a campground," Cici said quietly, "Come on!"

Liam was not in a hurry, however. He wanted to find out who was sitting around the fire before they showed themselves.

"We have the advantage of darkness," he said. "What if they're criminals? What if they are hiding from the police? Or maybe they've escaped from prison."

Cici agreed and moved slowly to the light. But when they actually got close to the edge of the fire, Cici's laughter gave them away. The people sitting around the fire were actors. She could recognize Lucas Rivers in a shiny space suit. Around him were the cast of Space Traveler, and at their feet, an ice chest, and that meant only one thing: water.

"Hey guys," she said leading Liam into the circle of light. "We are so glad to see you! You are about to save our lives!"

UNIT 7

LISTENING page 47

E=Eileen   S=Stella

E   So what are we doing today, Stella?

S   I don't know. I hate my hair.

E   Why? You've got great hair.

S   No, I don't. It's so curly. It just sticks out of my head all over the place.

E   I have a lot of clients who would love to have curls like these.

S   Well, Eileen, I need your advice. I have to give a presentation tomorrow, and I want to look professional. The way I look at the moment, people are going to think I stuck my finger in a light socket, especially with this weather!

E   Okay, so it sounds like you want to have it straightened.

S   Oh, Eileen! Can you do that?

E   I can, but I always recommend trying the look first before we make a permanent change to a client's hair.

S   Let's do it, then.

E   Wait, wait. We need to talk about the cut.

S   You're the expert. What do you think?

E   Usually about shoulder length works for straight hair. It's a very polished look.

S   I like that. There's a woman at my office with a cut like that. She always looks perfect, but do you think it would look good on me?

E   Sure, as long as we don't go too short.

S   What about the color?

E   Well, we could do some highlights or something dramatic.

S   I'm not sure about dramatic. I want it to look natural.

E   Okay, what if we just do a few highlights to brighten it up a bit.

S   Good.

E   So here's the plan. I'll cut your hair to about here, add a few highlights to bring out the gold, and then I can blow it out to make it straight for a couple of days. You can see how you like it and let me know if you want to make the change permanent. Does that sound good?

S   Will it stay straight until tomorrow?

E   Of course. Trust me. I've done this before.

S   Are you sure, because this is a really important presentation.

E   Just relax and leave it to me.

S   Okay, I'm in your hands.

E   There you go, now let's go get you shampooed, and I'll get started.

LISTENING PLUS page 47

E=Eileen   S=Stella

E   So Stella, what do you think?

S   Wow Eileen...

E   Do you like it?

S   I look so different. My coworkers aren't going to recognize me.

E   Sure they will. Here look at the back.

S   I can't believe how straight it is.

E   Well, that's what you asked for, and do you see the color. It's still the same, very natural just a little brighter, which works with straight hair.

S   I see it.

E   It goes well with your skin. See, look at your eyes.

S   And it's so much shorter. Look at all that hair on the floor.

E   Right, that's what you wanted, isn't it?

S   It is what I wanted, but...

E   You don't like it?

S   No, I do! I do like it. I like it a lot. I just have to get used to the new me.

E   Whew, you had me worried for a minute. But I have to say, I think you look very professional.

S   I feel professional. Thank you, Eileen.

E   My pleasure!

UNIT 8

LISTENING page 53

A=Alan   P=Paula   M=Mike   R=Rosie

A   Hello neighbors! Can I have your attention please? Tonight's town hall meeting is about the city's very exciting proposal to redesign Marshall Street. Here to explain this plan is Paula Wallace, an urban planner and consultant on the project. Welcome Paula.

P   Thank you Alan. Hello everyone, I'd like to begin with a show of hands. If streets were safer for pedestrians, would you approve? Good. Now, if streets were safer for bicycles, would you approve? Great! Now if streets had less congestion, would you approve? And finally, if buses came on time, would you approve? I see lots of hands, out there! Fantastic! Those are all the goals of the Marshall Street project.

M   I have a question.

P   Yes? Go ahead, sir.

M   I heard you are going to close off Marshall Street to cars.

P   That's only partly true. Our plan is to reduce the vehicle lanes from four lanes to two.

M   How is that going to make things better? Wouldn't closing a lane make traffic worse?

P   Let me explain the proposal, and I think it will make more sense. This proposal follows a Complete Streets Model, which means including all types of transportation. Currently, Marshall has four lanes for vehicle traffic. The plan is to reduce vehicle lanes to two. That would provide space for a designated bus lane, a protected bike lane, and wider sidewalks.

M   But that's impossible! You can't do that. Marshall Street would become more crowded than ever!

P   Actually, we've done a study of traffic flow patterns in urban areas, and in most cases, the traffic doesn't get worse. That's because drivers who are not going to stop anyway, will use other streets where there are fewer bicycles and pedestrians.

R   I like this plan, Mike. I use my bicycle to get to campus every day, and I'm always afraid I'm going to get killed.

M   But Rosie! I have a shop on Marshall Street. If you make cars take a different street, I'll lose customers. So will all the other businesses on Marshall!

LISTENING PLUS page 53

A=Alan   P=Paula   M=Mike   R=Rosie

A   Please, everyone, let's give Ms. Wallace a chance to explain. Go ahead, Paula.

P   Actually, a Complete Streets Model should improve the local economy.

M   But how? I sell flowers! People drive to my store.

P   I understand. But our studies show that most traffic on Marshall Street does not stop. It passes right through the neighborhood. Now, what is your name, sir?

M   Mike.

P   Mike, I think it's wonderful that you sell flowers. A flower shop is extremely good for a neighborhood economy by making it a nice place to walk. And where there are pedestrians, businesses grow.

For example, what if a nice cafe with outdoor tables opened next to your flower shop? You could sell to the restaurant *and* its customers.

M   Yeah, if! But how will people get there if you start closing lanes?

P   In a Complete Streets Model, not all your customers will be drivers. If Marshall Street is more interesting and attractive than the other streets, it will be more pedestrian-friendly. And I have some interesting information that supports this plan. An apartment building is going up on Marshall and 19th. The parking entrance will be on Field Street, and the pedestrian entrance will be on Marshall. The builders are directing residents to walk by your shop!

R   And if the street is a little quieter and the environment a little cleaner, they'll stop and buy flowers on the way home! I think it'll be good for your business.

M   Okay, okay, That's a good point. I'll think about it.

P   I'm really glad you asked, Mike! I'm sure other business owners feel the same way! I'll be happy to send you some studies on other Complete Streets projects.

M   It just might work. I'm glad I came tonight.

UNIT 9

LISTENING page 59

1. **M**=Mina   **K**=Kim

M   Kim, I need to talk to you.

K   Oh. Hi Mina! What is it?

M   I heard Jeff talking on the phone. I think he found out we were trying to get those two customers to go on a date.

K   Who?

M   You know, Mr. Sanchez and Ms. O'Reilly? They always come in here to print their menus.

K   Oh them! How did he find out?

M   I don't know, but he's the boss, and he always knows everything that happens in this place.

K   He's probably mad.

M   Yeah, we shouldn't have told Mr. Sanchez about Ms. O'Reilly.

K   And you definitely shouldn't have given him her number.

M   Well, they seemed like a good match.

K   Yeah, but what do we do now? Do you think Jeff is really upset?

M   I don't know.

2. **P**=Pablo   **E**=Eric

P   Hey, Eric! I looked for you at Cathy's birthday party. Why weren't you there?

E   I wasn't invited.

P   You're joking. Aren't you and Cathy like best friends?

E   Well, not at the moment. Apparently, she's kind of irritated with me.

P   Why?

E   Well, she found out I went to the beach without her.

P   Really? That's not a big deal.

E   I told her I was going to the library. I shouldn't have done that.

P   Let me guess. She found out.

E   Yeah, she was at the library looking for me.

P   Yeah, I would have told her the truth. Why didn't you just ask her to go with you?

E   I was going with some of my basketball friends, and Cathy hates basketball. I didn't want it to be uncomfortable.

P   Yeah, but you're paying for it now. The party was fun. You would have enjoyed it.

3. **B**=Belle   **A**=Andrew

B   Andrew, what's up?

A   Nothing.

B   Aw, come on. You have a worried look on your face.

A   I had a chance to go to a new technology convention in Denver, and I said I couldn't go.

B   Oh, why did you do that?

A   Well, the truth is, I'm afraid of flying. I hate airplanes.

B   Really, that's not good for a guy who does technical support for a big national company.

A   I know. I should have gone, but I was nervous.

B   How are you going to overcome your fear? You can't stop traveling.

A   I realize that. I've decided to take a class to help me overcome my fear of flying.

B   Good, just think how much better you'll feel.

A   I should have taken one a long time ago!

B   Don't be too hard on yourself. You'll go to the next convention.

LISTENING PLUS page 59

1. **J**=Jeff   **K**=Kim

J   Kim, one of our customers told me you and Mina offered to give him another customer's phone number.

K   I'm sorry. I don't remember, but I didn't give him anyone's phone number.

J   Then how did he get Frances O'Reilly's number?

K   I don't know, ask Mina. Perhaps she gave it to him.

J   Well, it doesn't really matter who gave it to him. It was very unprofessional. You shouldn't have interfered in our customers' personal lives.

K   I realize that now. Mina and I just thought they would get along.

J   Well, don't do it again. It could have become uncomfortable between them and then we would have lost two customers!

K   I'm sorry. I won't do it again.

2. **E**=Eric   **C**=Cathy

E   Hi, Cathy.

C   Hi, Eric.

E   Happy birthday! I heard you had a good party yesterday.

C   Yep.

E   Look, I know you're mad at me. I should have told you I was going to the beach.

C   I don't know why you didn't.

E   I just thought it would be easier at the time.

C   Easier? Why?

E   Well, it's hard to bring friends together if they don't know each other.

C   So why didn't you just say that! You're a free person. I wouldn't have minded.

E   I know. You're a good friend. I'm sorry.

C   It's okay but promise to be honest with me next time.

E   I promise. So, are we still friends?

C   I guess.

E   Whew!

3. **B**=Belle   **A**=Andrew

B   Andrew! I haven't seen you for a while. How are you? Did you take that fear of flying class?

A   Yes! And it worked. I went on a work trip to Philadelphia.

B   You did? And how did it go?

A   I was still nervous at first, but then I realized something.

B   What was that?

A   That being afraid isn't going to change anything. After that I was fine.

B   Good for you! So now you can go anywhere you want.

A   Yes, there's another convention in Florida next month, and I've already gotten my ticket.

UNIT 10

LISTENING page 67

C=Carolina   DH=Dr. Howard   DC=Dr. Chin

C   Secret organizations are controlling our lives. Aliens may have landed in the desert, and mad scientists are planning to take over the world. This is the stuff of movies, but for some people, stories like these are real.
Welcome to Mysteries of the Mind where we look at human behavior. In today's show, our speakers will discuss conspiracy theorists, those are people who believe that hidden forces are affecting our lives. Today I have two sociologists, Dr. Jenna Howard, and Dr. Luis Chin who are here to tell us more about it. Welcome, and let's start with you Dr. Howard. How do we recognize a conspiracy theorist?

DH   Well, people are all different as you know, but we've identified three characteristics that most conspiracy theorists share. The first one is that these people don't just want an explanation. They need one. When something happens, they start connecting information to build a story. It might be wrong or even fake information, but they don't fact-check it.

C   But why not?

DC   As Dr. Howard says, they could have put so much energy into their theory that they refuse to believe details that challenge it. Typically, they'll argue that research studies must have been organized by the conspirators.

C   Even when everyone agrees it is scientific evidence?

DC   Even scientific evidence. Take medicine as an example. There may have been hundreds of scientific studies that prove that a medicine is safe. However, many people, educated people, still refuse to take the medicine because they believe there is a conspiracy to hide the negative side effects. If a conspiracy theorist gets a fever after taking some medicine, that person could think, "It must have been the medicine that caused the fever." In reality, it is likely that the two things are not connected.

C   I like to think I would believe scientific evidence.

DC   We all would, but over and over again we find that presenting conspiracy theorists with facts just doesn't work. It often does the opposite. They find other people who don't believe the facts either. This is the second characteristic. Conspiracy theorists find each other and form a community.

C   But doesn't belief in a false story cause problems?

DC   Absolutely! It causes major problems. When groups of people make decisions based on false claims, there can be negative consequences. Here's another example. The World Health Organization has recommended that people shouldn't eat a lot of meat. However, conspiracy theorists can find sites on the Internet that say this health recommendation is an anti-meat conspiracy. It was started by the vegetable industry as a way for farmers to sell more corn or broccoli or whatever. Conspiracy theorists will find these websites and treat their false claims as the truth.

DH   Yes, and that leads to the third characteristic, which is a need to feel special. Conspiracy theorists like thinking they know something that other people don't. There is a lot of scientific evidence that vegetables are good for us, but conspiracy theorists think they've found a hidden truth that no one else knows.

C   But what if the conspiracy is real? What if these people really do uncover secret plans?

DC   Good point! I'm glad you brought that up. As responsible social scientists, we have to accept that sometimes conspiracy theories are not just made up stories. Sometimes there is a real conspiracy.

C So how do we tell the difference?

DH The most important thing is learn how to recognize useful information from false claims. People need to check the websites and publications to make sure the information comes from a research university or a scientific organization. The truth is out there, but it's complex.

LISTENING PLUS page 67

C=Carolina **B**=Bill **DH**=Dr. Howard **DC**=Dr. Chin

C And now let's take a few calls. If you've just joined us, we are here with Dr. Chin and Dr. Howard, two experts on conspiracy theorists. They've been discussing the characteristics of people who continue to believe something even when there is little or no evidence to support it. We have Bill on the line. Welcome to Mysteries of the Mind, Bill.

B Hello Carolina, thanks for having me.

C What is on your mind today?

B I'm calling in because I do a lot of research on the Internet, myself. I think it's very important to know what's really happening in the world.

DC Yes, well the Internet definitely makes information gathering easy, but you have to be careful. People can be tricked into believing false information.

B That's what I'm calling about. I have a question.

C Go ahead.

B What if your information about meat is wrong?

C What do you mean?

B Well, you said the anti-meat movement is a fake story, but what if it's not. What if there really is an organized effort to force people to eat more vegetables. What about that?

DH Ahh, well Bill, The World Health Organization is fairly well respected. However, you could fact check by looking at medical journals. I always say, if in doubt, always check, and maybe you'll learn something useful.

B Yes, but don't you agree that these journals could have published the wrong information?

DC Ahhh, Dr. Howard and I are not experts on diet and nutrition, but many experts from different organizations review journal articles. They couldn't all have been part of the conspiracy. I have to say, I think it's important for all of us to recognize that sometimes we only choose to believe information that fits our story or theory.

B That's what I'm worried about. You believe vegetables are safe and healthy, but my friends and I know the truth.

C Well, Bill, thanks for calling. Let's go to our next caller.

UNIT 11

LISTENING page 73

R=Renee **P**=Pete

R Today on *What's New*, we talk to Pete Bretis. Pete works for the magazine *Inventor Today*, and he's written the cover story on this year's invention awards. Pete, welcome to the program.

P Hi Renee, it's a pleasure to be here.

R Give us a little background, Pete. How did you choose the winners?

P We gave prizes to inventions that really made a difference in people's lives.

R I see. So what made the list?

P A cooking pot.

R What?

P Yes, I know what you're thinking, Renee, but this pot is smart. It's called the Chef Pot because it is a chef and a pot in one. It has sensors that gather information, and it tells you what to do.

R Wow! That's ingenious. If I'd had a pot like that when my kids were young, I wouldn't have burned so many meals!

P Exactly! That's why it won an award. It makes life easier.

R So any other gadgets?

P Yes, robots. We had to give an award to a robot. Inventors are doing amazing things with them these days! We found a team of inventors in Canada with an interesting idea. They created Friendix. Friendix is a small robot with a personality.

R Do you mean like a digital assistant?

P Yes, but this one can move. It can talk to you and connect with the Internet, AND it can move. In fact, it will follow you around the house. The really cool thing is that it has cameras and sensors, so when you are not home, it can move around the house and show you what it sees—you just need to download a special app to your phone. And get this: you can speak through it! It can even let someone in the door if they've forgotten their key.

R How futuristic!

P Well, it's still not able to do things like load the dishwasher, but it can dance if you ask it to. We think it's a great digital companion.

R Wow. I wish I had had something like that when I was a kid. Was the robot the winner?

P It was near the top. We actually gave first place to an invention that saves lives. It's a tiny, inexpensive medical device. It's called the Mini-Medi Lab. It can test for diseases in places without hospitals or power, and it doesn't need electric power.

R It doesn't need electricity? How does it work?

P You turn a handle to power it. That means it's affordable and portable. The inventors were doctors, and they said that if they had invented it ten years ago, they could have saved over a million lives in places that are far away from hospitals.

R That sounds like a really important invention, Pete. Thank you for sharing!

LISTENING PLUS page 73

R=Renee P=Pete C=Caller L=Larry

R Looks like we have callers. Hello, caller, you are on the line.

C Hi, I want to ask Pete a question. What advice do you have for new inventors?

P Find a community. There are places called maker spaces in many cities. They have machines and tools. When you join the maker space, you usually have to pay, but then you can use the equipment to work on your invention. You also meet people who can help you.

C I'll do that. Thank you.

R Here's another; Larry, you are on the line.

L Hi, Pete, I have an idea for an invention, but I am afraid someone might steal it.

P Let me ask you a question, Larry. Can you make the invention by yourself?

L Um, not at the moment, no.

P Then you have two choices: One, you can figure out how to make it.

L How do I do that?

P Learn the skills and maybe buy some tools. Or, two, you can bring in partners who have the skills, money, or tools. There are thousands of ideas out there, Larry, but an idea by itself is not enough. You have to be able to build the thing.

L I see.

P Don't give up Larry!

UNIT 12

LISTENING page 79

A=Announcer S=Sergio

A Next up, the local news with Sergio Tucker.

S Our top story tonight is an update on the Serena Novak rescue. The five-year-old was walking with her grandmother when she fell into a hole. Rescuers have been working all night. They want to make the opening wider so they can lower an emergency worker down to get the kindergartener. In a press conference, Sheriff Eleanor Jones told reporters that recent rains have made the ground soft, so they have to work carefully. They do not want more dirt to fall on the little girl. So far, they've been able to lower a flashlight and warm clothing to Serena who is alive and unhurt. We'll have more updates for you as the story continues.
In other news, medical centers are reporting several hospitalizations due to a mysterious illness. Doctors say that patients are coming to emergency rooms with dizziness, fevers, and upset stomachs. So far the disease does not appear to be life-threatening, but doctors are asking anyone with symptoms to call the centers for disease control. They are not sure what causes the illness, but they are running some tests.
Our next story takes us downtown where angry protesters are fighting to save the historic Central Library. Police report that more than 300 people lined the streets on Prescott Boulevard to oppose a plan to tear down the nearly 100-year-old building. The crowd includes librarians, teachers, and local citizens who joined the historic preservation society in a march to city hall. They stood on the steps and gave speeches about the role and value of the building, which was designed by Alfie Chang in 1926. In a public statement, library board member Jeff Roberts, said that while the board members understand the public's love for the building, they feel it has become too expensive to repair. In the meantime, the public is invited to post comments on the library's website.

LISTENING PLUS page 79

S=Sergio

S And now the late night round up on today's news. The sheriff's office has reported that little Serena Novak has been brought to the surface and is now safely in the arms of her parents, Avery and Brita Novak. The girl is muddy and a little frightened but she was quoted as saying that the first thing she wanted was a hamburger, French fries, and a chocolate milkshake. It turns out that she and her grandmother were on their way to lunch when she fell in the hole, and she hadn't forgotten grandma's promise.
Doctors at Mercy Hospital have found the source of the mysterious illness to a type of bacteria that got into Flavor Chip ice cream. The condition is not contagious as they had previously thought, but experts at the centers for disease control are saying that anyone who bought Flavor Chip should not eat it as it may be infected with the bacteria. Grocery stores are removing Flavor chip from the shelves until further notice.
We've also got an update on the Alfie Chang library. Apparently, opponents of the proposal to tear down the library learned of a secret meeting among board members at the home of Jeff Roberts. Over 50 people blocked the street outside his home calling for a change in the plan. Police were called to the scene, but no arrests were made. The historic preservation society said that they have filed a lawsuit against the board, so the building is safe for now. For more on this story and other local news, tune in for the midnight news with my colleague, Anna Barkley.

VOCABULARY

UNIT 1

collect comic books
do volunteer work
draw cartoons
go for hikes
make videos
play the violin
run marathons
take selfies

collect autographs
do martial arts
do yoga
play music
take classes
take photos

does martial arts
makes costumes
plans bicycle tours

aerial
capture
contests
eventually
landscapes
navigate
range
tropical

UNIT 2

cartoon
documentary
drama
game show
music video
news program
sports program
talk show

cooking show
crime series
reality show
romantic comedy
sitcom
travel show

arrest
investigation
robbery

affordable
characteristics
followers
influencers
marketing
merchandise
platforms
responses
vlog

UNIT 3

abstract painting
drawing
installation
landscape
mural
portrait
sculpture
still life

ancient
boring
colorful
graffiti
illustration
photography
pottery
powerful
realistic
statue
traditional
wild

anthropology exhibit
pop culture museum
sculpture park

expeditions
frames
paste
pasted
suffering
violence
inspires

UNIT 4

clumsy
creative
generous
organized
reserved
talkative

charming
cautious
insecure
nerdy
optimistic
outgoing

adventurous

circumstances
emotional
events
fluid
inner
loyal
outer
reconnected
vital

UNIT 5

digital assistant
game console
smartphone
smartwatch
sports camera
tablet
virtual reality goggles
wireless headphones

browse
downloaded
features

addictions
chemical
device
impulses
notification
observing
pleasure
psychologists
releases

UNIT 6

angry
careless
cheerful
in a hurry
noisy
patient

anxious about her baby
enthusiastic about music
late for a flight
reluctant to say goodbye

access
cozy
delighted
deserve
downside
fine dining
hosts
paradise

UNIT 7

cut
dyed
highlights
manicure
pierced
shaved
straightened
trimmed

accessories
blow out
curly
polished

apparently
chic
faith
loose
plaid
spouse
subtle
wardrobe

UNIT 8

art scene
bike lanes
nightlife
pedestrians
public transportation
vehicle traffic

air quality
cost of living
crime rate
housing prices
job opportunities
public parks
school system
shops and restaurants

designated bus lanes
pedestrian-friendly
   sidewalks
protected bicycle lanes
vehicle lanes

care providers
elderly
empathy
expose
intergenerational
lap
participants
retirement
rewarding
stuck

UNIT 9

amused
confused
embarrassed
inconsiderate
irritated
sympathetic

grateful
helpful
hurt
relieved
rude
shocked
thoughtful
uncomfortable

confidence
honest
interfere
overcome

burst into tears
excuse
graduation
homeless
painful
regret
thoughtless
unpleasant

UNIT 10

conspiracy theory
doctored photo
fact-checker
hoax
mystery
prediction

evidence
explanation
fact
myth
proof
rumor
scam
urban legend

false claims
hidden forces
negative consequences
authentic
dismiss
fooled
pretended
visible

UNIT 11

appliance
gadget
gear
instrument
tool
utensil

adapt
breakthrough
contraption
create
device
develop
improve
innovate

futuristic
ingenious
portable
practical

artificial
collaboration
efficient
expertise
exploration
repurpose
solar panels
specialize

UNIT 12

article
breaking news
camera operator
citizen journalist
headline
news site
reporter
weather report

blogger
broadcast
business
column
editor
journalist
politics
update

contagious
oppose
protesters
rescue

attraction
consequences
curiosity
negativity bias
overall
satisfies
survival
trust